CONTINENTAL DIVIDE
PACIFIC   ATLANTIC

Twenty-nine Hills

A Great Divide mountain bike epic

GW00801893

by Marty Basch
with recipes by Jan Duprey

Top of the World Communications
Center Conway, New Hampshire

Twenty-nine Hills
By Marty Basch

Published by:
Top of the World Communications
PO Box 105, Center Conway, NH 03813

Copyright © 2005 by Marty Basch
Printed in the United States of America
Library of Congress Control Number: 2004098876
ISBN 0-9646510-3-3

Cover design and book layout by Al Hospers
     (www.cambersoft.com)
Map by Adventure Cycling Association
     (www.adventurecycling.com)

Cover photo by Marty Basch
     (www.martybasch.com)
Photos by Marty Basch and Jan Duprey (page 95)
Recipes by Jan Duprey

To Jan,
You did it

ACKNOWLEDGMENTS

The road is always long and thanks are many. Always, thanks to family, friends and those who helped us along the way. Before we hit the road, thanks to Terry Love and Bob Sullivan at Sports Outlet in North Conway, N.H., BOB Trailer's Philip Novotny and Jeff Welt at L.L. Bean. Thanks to the media who helped us tell this story while we were rolling: Jay O'Neal(RIP my friend), Amy Mahoney, Alan Greenwood, Jill Hodges, Jeff Gutridge, George Cleveland, Mark Guerringue and Adam Hirshan. Kevin Murphy, once again, proved to be a technological lifeline.

Adventure Cycling Association's Mike "Mac" McCoy and Teri Maloughney were excellent resources. The insights of Elaine and John Doyle were most welcome. Al Hospers was an ace in the graphics department.

The Great Divide Mountain Bike Route

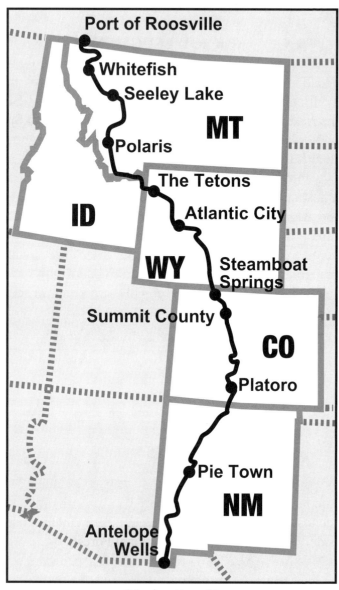

Port of Roosville

Whitefish

Seeley Lake

MT

Polaris

The Tetons

Atlantic City

ID

WY

Steamboat Springs

Summit County

CO

Platoro

Pie Town

NM

Antelope Wells

(Map is not to scale)

TABLE OF CONTENTS

Recipes

Chapter One

Somewhere in Montana

Dinner didn't sound all that good. After bicycling nearly 40 miles on dirt, sand, gravel, and rutted roads while being chased by hordes of hungry deer and horse flies, you develop quite the appetite. Plus, the July sun pelted down through the vents of our bike helmets frying our brains with summer heat. To make it more uncomfortable, my thighs were on fire, forever-protesting my decision to try to pedal over 2,500 miles on a mountain bike from Canada to Mexico.

"Ever hear of an engine?," I imagined them asking me.

After such a day, the way to end it would be in an air-conditioned motel with a gloriously long and hot shower. The motel would be across the street from a steakhouse with an all-you-can-eat salad bar and the thighs would protest no more in making frequent trips from the booth to the bar for another heaping of potato salad, three bean salad, and cherry tomatoes that go squish in your mouth.

This was not to be. We were in western Montana's Centennial Valley and miles away from civilization: flush toilets, restaurants, motel, and grocery store. Lima, a small town off the interstate where we had started out from that day, had all those luxurious necessities. We were stocked with food like pasta, tomato sauce, tuna fish, Spam, and ramen noodles all carried with our gear in one-wheel trailers behind our mountain bikes.

1

MARTY BASCH

I pedaled up to Jan, dwarfed by the huge jagged-topped mountain range on the Montana-Idaho border, and asked her what was for dinner.

"Star-spangled Spam," she said.

Food is Jan's passion. She's a chef, a pint-sized wunderkind who is as quick with a knife as a cowboy is on the draw. Jan knows food and could even turn cubes of wonder-meat into something tasty. She introduced me once to a Hawaiian dish called a musubi, a Spam and rice sandwich wrapped in seaweed complete with various spices.

If you're hungry, it's quite good.

I was hungry. So Spam it was going to be.

Star-spangled Spam turned out to be the featured dish at an impromptu trailside outdoor dinner theater.

This was our last night in Montana, riding day 21 of our trip along the Great Divide Mountain Bike Route. For nearly a month, we had ridden through the beauty of the "Big Sky" state and seen its idiosyncrasies as well from bullet-ridden street signs to an interstate with no speed limit. It was a place with more barbs on fences than people who tended them.

But the sky was bold, limitless and blue. North-facing ravines held snow in the mountains even through summer's wrath. Bear paraded through the woods. Awe-inspiring panoramas followed many corners we rounded on our bikes.

Montana had been filled with surprises and it was about to unleash one more smack in our faces.

Riding for much of the day, Jan and I started looking for a place to camp. She was tired. I was tired. There always seemed to be one more hill to conquer, another mile to go before the right place to spend the night appeared. From our bike seats, we looked for that flat swatch of land that would hold us and our tent. Hopefully it would be by a creek, or "crik" as it was heard by these East Coast ears. The land had to be federal land, Bureau of Land Management (BLM) property. That way we wouldn't be trespassing, and we had already learned Montana folks will speak up if you're on their land without permission.

2

By a t-junction and near a gate, we found BLM land, government land many local old timers called it. It was our ticket to free camping.

Behind a fence and by a creek, Jan and I quickly went into our routine of setting up camp. With military precision, the tent went up, the sleeping bags and pads were unfurled, the gear was stored safely by the tent, the stove was assembled, and water began to simmer for tea. Even after a hard day in the bike saddle, Jan likes to cook and she set out to prepare the inaugural version of

STAR-SPANGLED SPAM

Ingredients:
1 can Spam Luncheon Meat
1/2 pound mini-star pasta
1 can stewed tomatoes
2 teaspoons dry basil
2 teaspoons dehydrated garlic flakes
Grated cheese to taste

Directions:
Dice the Spam. Cook star pasta. Stars will cook quickly. Drain and set aside. Sauté the diced Spam. Add basil, minced garlic and can of tomatoes. Toss together with stars, reheat if needed. Top with your favorite grated cheese.

Star-spangled Spam. While cycling, the idea hit her to combine squares of wonder-meat, tomato sauce, and small stars of pasta all in one pot.

When it's the only game in town, Star-spangled Spam can be gloriously tasty. It was that night. We were taking a break from wolfing it down, when the stillness of the evening was broken by distant moos, honks, and slobbering. We didn't know it immediately but Montana was about to throw us a going away party. A hulking mass moved toward us from the horizon down the needle-straight dirt road edged with sagebrush. The road passed directly in front of the tent and safety was ensured by the fence.

"Jan, is it my imagination or are those cows coming our way?," I asked.

Jan concurred that was exactly what was happening.

We had company for dinner. The herd became tangible. Hundreds of cattle - brown, white, and black - were being paraded down the road by bona fide, whip-snapping, lasso-carrying cowboys hollering and whistling at the huffing heifers.

Jan and I turned out to have front row seats for a live version of Montana dinner theater. From the safety of the fence, we watched in wonder as the herd kicked up dust and rumbled by. Horns, heads, and hides dominated the landscape as the ensemble ambled forth. A few of the younger, hipper bovines sported earrings. Lots had tattoos.

We scrambled for our cameras to record this genuine cattle drive that was happening right in front of our tent. You just don't get this kind of entertainment back in our home state of New Hampshire. It was like we were out of our element and hoisted into a scene from "City Slickers" where a few New York friends head west for a dude ranch vacation and end up leading a cattle drive. Too bad comic actor Billy Crystal wasn't around to join in.

Lights! Cameras! Action! This was better than scoring two-for-one seats in New York's Time Square for a Broadway musical. The sounds, smells, and special effects of the drive were just feet from us as we recorded the drive with cameras while wondering if they planned to swing open that gate and march right into our front yard.

That didn't happen. Two, three, four cowboys kept the herd rolling under the clear Montana sky. One errant young critter didn't feel much like complying and jumped the fence a few feet from the tent. Jan

The cattle drives are real in Montana.

and I were just transfixed. As if they were cued by a director, one cowboy jumped the fence to capture the fleeing future Spam ingredient. Maybe, because the cowboy saw the cameras or maybe, because that's what a cowboy does in such a situation, he unhitched his rope, held it high above his head, and tried to lasso the escapee. He came up short and the cow jumped back over the fence followed by the cowboy.

When all was in order, the cowboy moseyed on over to us on horseback.

"Sorry for disturbing your peace and quiet," he said.

Disturbing? Was he kidding?

"No problem," I replied. "Couldn't get tickets for something like this if we tried."

We exchanged further pleasantries and he tipped his hat before riding off into the sunset as the stage soon faded to the twinkling stars and black of a Montana night.

Chapter Two

Before you go: North Conway, New Hampshire

"You stink."

These were the first words out of Jan's mouth after I returned from biking above the Arctic Circle in 1996. I was hoping for "I love you."

I had spent three satisfying months on a solo bicycle trip in the Scandinavian Arctic and Jan met me at Boston's Logan Airport. We had been dating for a couple of years and I was yearning for clear, unaccented English and a quick change out - with Jan's help - from my smelly clothes which I had lived in since leaving Norway.

Somewhere along the 11-hour boat ride, 18-hour train excursion, 17-hour wait for my bicycle that wasn't on the same train I was on, and eight hours on various planes, I forgot to change my shirt, pants and underwear so Jan's words may have reeked a tad of truth.

Being a lovely and compassionate person, Jan did follow through with an "I love you," threw in an "I missed you," and then uttered the prophetic "I'm going on the next bike trip."

For the record, my first words to Jan were something along the lines of "I love you, I miss you, what's for dinner, and I hope it's not mackerel in tomato sauce."

Jan's announcement she would be going on the next bike

trip stayed with me long after the three-hour drive back to the mountains of New Hampshire. Jan on a bike trip would be a wonderful thing. She certainly deserved it, having put up with me in one form or another for three years, rallying back from her divorce, and raising her teenage daughter. Adventure called her name. For one summer, she could travel through America's heart, live on ramen noodles, sleep in the woods, and wear the same clothes for days. We could stink together.

Since I was a teenager, bike trips have been a part of my life. There was summer camp for a few years, but when I turned 15, I took to the road in an organized bicycling trip along Cape Cod in Massachusetts. Independence and adventure teamed up on me and hooked me on two-wheel travel.

This stayed with me into adulthood. When the 1990s hit and I entered my 30s, laptop computers and the Internet combined to make it possible to go on bike trips with a link to the world. Being a writer, I worked along the way, filing stories about my experiences.

Jan's been supportive of this ever since we met over a seven-layer dip at a party in 1993. I remember what we were eating because Jan remembers. When she recalls an event, chances are she'll be able to serve up at least one meal from memory of that day too.

She's no slouch either. An avid skier, she's also at home on the hiking trails. She already had proven herself on a bicycle too, surviving a couple of cold, spring tandem trips that combined skiing, snowboarding and cycling.

With a borrowed baby buggy transformed into a ski and snowboard gear shuttle, we once rode about 175 miles from Sugarloaf/USA in Carrabassett Valley, Maine to Sunday River in Newry, Maine. Then it was on to New Hampshire and the Wildcat Ski Area, directly across from the Northeast's highest peak Mount Washington. To finish things off, we pedaled to North Conway and schussed the trails at Cranmore Mountain Resort. We didn't camp out in tents, but slept indoors at hotels. We braved snow, cold, and the slushy spray from passing motor vehicles while wearing

MARTY BASCH

helmets, face masks, and goggles as we rode.

Despite the mind-numbing cold, we decided to do it again.
So the next year, we covered a 100 mile loop through the White
Mountains. The bike path through Franconia Notch State Park was
still frozen and being used as a snowmobile trail, so we rode on the
interstate's shoulder as huge trucks whizzed by. It snowed so much
one morning we had to wait for the plow guys to clear the roads
before we started riding again. This time we stayed at condos and a
new form of camping was discovered: condo camping.

After that, we both had enough of riding in New England's
cold and snow. The novelty ran its course. Jan was ready for a
summer ride.

She knew what it would be like. In 1994, I road my bicycle
from Maine to Alaska. Jan got a taste of the road by following me
from time to time in her SUV. The trip began in Portland, Maine
about 60 miles east of our home so for the first few days I was
close enough for her to find me after she got off from work. She
was the roving support team. During her days off, she drove as far
as Ontario to make sure all was well. When the driving took up too
much time, she took a few days off and flew out to Manitoba and
we traveled together, she in a rental car.

This got us talking about doing a big bike trip together one day.

Enter the creation of the Great Divide Mountain Bike Route.
Being members of the Missoula, Montana-based Adventure
Cycling Association which was mapping out the route along the
Rockies, we followed the route's development through the pages of
the Association's magazine, *Adventure Cyclist*.

Jan had a knack for swiping the magazine from my night stand
and reading the latest report about its' progress. It was during one
of those sessions that Jan put down the magazine, gazed lovingly
into my eyes and cooed "Honey." From that moment on, I knew I
was being drafted for some kind of service.

Whenever Jan starts a sentence like that it usually means I end
up saying, "Yes Honey, whatever you want." This doesn't always
happen immediately. Sometimes it takes days, hours or minutes.
This time, it took seconds.

"Let's really do this," she said.

"Yes Honey, whatever you want," I said.

From that moment on, the Great Divide Mountain Bike Route became a fixture in our lives. On paper, the route stretches 2,470 miles along the Continental Divide, a ridge of the Rocky Mountains which forms a natural watershed, and separates rivers flowing east from those streaming west. With a combination of fire access roads, jeep trails, occasional paved roads and singletrack, the route winds through Montana, Idaho, Wyoming, Colorado and New Mexico. Is there a change in elevation? You bet. Eureka, Montana owns the low point at 2,577 feet while Colorado claims the high point at 11,900.

Challenges? Ask Michael "Mac" McCoy. He was Adventure Cycling Association's national coordinator for the Great Divide Mountain Bike Route. He not only mapped it out, but also helped conceive and research the route. If there was a man who could give advice about what waited for us in the West, he was it. So I called him at his home in Idaho and peppered him with questions from the route's history to its most remote section.

"There is a 130 mile stretch in Wyoming between Atlantic City and Rawlins with no services," he said. "It's wide open, arid, sagebrush-covered, with no trees. Wild horses run through there. It can be windy. This is the area called the Great Divide Basin, where the Continental Divide splits and forms a circle where waters don't drain to the east or west. They just sit and evaporate. It's big, probably over 100 miles across."

McCoy relayed the creation of the Route. The seed was planted when McCoy read in an 1985 two-part magazine article about the exploits of two Laramie, Wyoming brothers - Mike and Dan Moe - who pedaled and pushed their bicycles along the rugged spine of the Continental Divide from Mexico to Canada.

Mountain biking was coming of age in the 1980s and bike touring was still mainly done by cyclists on paved roads riding thin-tired bicycles. The jump hadn't been realized to touring on dirt roads. McCoy's idea light came on when he read about the Moes.

"That sort of put the idea in the back of my mind," he said.

"As time progressed, mountain biking became more popular. It appeared to me that there was a major crevice between mountain biking and road touring. The two were separate sports. A person would go off on the trails and do day rides on a mountain bike, but touring bicycles were sticking to the paved roads."

The idea of mountain biking along the Divide on dirt roads stayed on McCoy's cerebral backburner for about five years. Mountain biking grew. In 1990, he and then Adventure Cycling Association executive director Gary MacFadden were sharing a meal at their favorite Mexican eatery in Missoula when the Divide mountain bike route idea was brought up again. They wanted to do it, but other projects took precedence.

In 1994, the timing finally clicked and McCoy spearheaded the effort to establish an official route along the Divide called the Great Divide Mountain Bike Route. He wrote about it in the pages of *Adventure Cyclist*. Just like McCoy had read about the Moes, the Moes now read about McCoy's project and sent a letter to him expressing their desire to help.

They were supposed to meet in Wyoming's Great Divide Basin in 1996 to figure out the way to cross.

But in September of 1995, the Moes died of hypothermia in an Arctic Ocean boating accident after their craft was capsized by a whale.

McCoy spent three years mapping the route, which was completed in 1997. The first official year to ride the Route was 1998.

Like McCoy, we needed a few things to come together before hitting the road. We needed a network of family and friends to take care of our home life and through them keep the domestic machine running during our absence. Jan's daughter needed supervision. The bills weren't going on vacation. Pay them. Mail must be picked up. Jan's employer guaranteed her job would be waiting for her when she got back.

The estimate for the trip was about $3,000 for the two of us. Being frugal people, it wasn't much of a challenge to save that amount. The key was to accumulate more than the estimated trip expenses for when the trip was over and re-enter the world of indoor plumbing, refrigeration and television.

But first we had some planning to do, which included taking a look at ourselves. This would be the longest time the two of us would go on an extended journey together. No buffers; warts and all. Ten years in age, one foot in height, and about 80 pounds of weight separated us. We were at different ends of the experience spectrum too. I had been traveling by bike for years, and Jan was still a relative rookie.

Jan was a 46 year-old single mom. I was a 36 year-old never-been-married guy.

Bike trips, to me, are symbols of freedom. During high school and college, vacations last for summer and there is plenty of time to roam the world. Then the career comes into play and touring takes a back seat to work and family. But there are exceptions. There's the engineer who can take a sabbatical and ride around for months on a bike. There are those who ride to ease the pain from divorce or celebrate a triumph over cancer. Over 20 and have a birthday ending in a zero? Hop on a bike.

This wasn't about any of that, it was about us, about adventure, about freedom of choice. For the first time in about 25 years, Jan would have a total summer vacation.

Together, we would pedal the miles and brave the hail. We would feel the exultation of reaching a summit, the pure joy of speed on the other side, and the tears of hope brought on by the trust of humanity when a stranger invites you into his home to rest from the road.

On the Divide, we would always be together.

That could be a problem too. Jan likes togetherness. I find the concept to be highly overrated at times and enjoy solitude as well. Jan likes togetherness so much she wanted to do the Divide on a tandem.

To discourage Jan, I conjured up a scenario where we hadn't showered for three days and I had eaten two bowls of chili for lunch. Would Jan want to share a tandem with me then?
She didn't! So single bikes it was.

First we needed to get new bikes. Gear talk doesn't thrill me all that much, but equipment is an essential part of any trip. Together, we had the basic gear for camping and touring. To level the playing field, I thought it would be a good idea to have the same kind of bike, both new, so that we would each be familiar with each other's rig when something went wrong.

I tried in vain to get corporate sponsorship for the trip, to find one company to underwrite the cost of the entire journey, including gear, food, transportation and lodging. I failed miserably in that quest, though I did get some tasty morsels. One company rejected the request, but did send us water bottles which I later re-gifted. L.L. Bean came through with products - clothing and tent - for us to test during our travels. Another company, BOB Trailers, gave us trailers in exchange for action photographs. Trailers were a Jan thing. After seeing them in a magazine, she declared, "Honey, we should use these." It didn't matter that I had used saddlebags for 20 years and thought they would do the trick.

As for the bikes, Jan the rookie came through for us. We went to Sports Outlet, a bike shop in North Conway, to shop for a bike. It was up to me to get us new bikes so it was time to fork over the credit card. We had been customers at the shop and knew the owners.

They had followed my previous cycling adventures and expressed enthusiasm about Jan and I riding together, so one of them said to Jan: "How about we sponsor you?"

Even though the question wasn't asked of me, I replied, "Uh, we need to talk about it."

Jan placed a rather strong grip on my elbow and led me to a corner of the store. She looked directly into my eyes and said, "Please explain to me exactly what it is that we need to talk about."

That's how we got new bikes.

An unorthodox piece of gear I carry is a laptop computer. Computer, discs, power supply, case and assorted other material - all wrapped in a dry bag - weighs about 10 pounds. It is an essential piece of equipment for me ever since I became a computer-carrying cycling guy in 1994 during the Maine to Alaska ride. On it, I keep a diary, expense records, and write stories.

For the Divide ride, two New Hampshire newspapers signed on for weekly stories: *The Nashua Telegraph* and *The Conway Daily Sun*. Both papers had taken my material before from the Alaska trip and the Arctic ride. The Sun also wanted weekly recipes from Jan, though Jan's experience in writing amounted to about the same experience I had as a chef. She became "One Pan Jan." She agreed to this after I told her she had already been signed up to do it. It made her nervous.

But not as nervous as when I told her she would also be writing for the ABC News web site, ABCNEWS.com. In addition to stories, photos and recipes, we would exchange e-mail with readers and if time permitted, have live chats on the web site.

The same stories that would appear in the newspapers, would also go on the New England Sports Network's web site, NESN.com. For a little audio, Jan and I planned to call, collect, both New Hampshire Public Radio (I called them during the Arctic ride too) and WMWV Radio in North Conway about every two weeks. We would do the same with the Resort Sports Network television affiliate in North Conway.

Jan's pre-trip planning also included being the resident pack rat. Unknown to me, Jan started to stock up on food about a year before we actually started the ride. She made care packages and had them sent to us from home during the ride. She even carried spices like oregano, salt, garlic, and pepper in small plastic containers. Jan knows how to make sushi. In one care package, she actually packed in the dry seaweed called nori needed to wrap sushi and make California rolls. She ended up sending the seaweed home during the trip when she realized it took less time to make ramen noodles after a 50 mile day on dirt roads than a sushi roll. After all, she had been rolling all day on the bike.

We also needed to order the six-map set for the Great Divide ride from Adventure Cycling. Jan wanted them one year before we were to go. I wanted the maps about a month before we hit the road. We compromised on six months. Ironically, not all the maps had been printed yet because the route was new and we didn't get the final two maps until about a month before the trip.

When we got the maps, Jan totally immersed herself in them and nearly every night went over the route, distances, and places to camp. The maps listed places to eat, lodging possibilities, and bike shop locations.

For me, planning for this trip was different from what I had done in the past. I wasn't used to following an established route. I wanted to make my own way, choose the roads I wanted to ride. For Jan, there was a sense of security knowing people expected to see bikers along the established route and that we would likely bump into the company of fellow Divide riders.

Jan and I also had opposing views on training for the trip. She believed in it. I didn't. So starting in April, about 10 weeks before the trip, she started riding in the cold, wet, and snowy New Hampshire spring. She rode with the trailer, getting used to it, and sometimes put weight in the rig to get a feel for the balance. She did have some experience pulling a trailer behind a bicycle. Not only did she survive those two snowy ski-carrying adventures, but she also worked for a couple of seasons for a delivery service pedaling packages around town with a cart in tow. About a month before we left, I started riding with her. There wasn't an established routine or anything. We would just ride on pavement, and in the sometimes muddy woods.

As the date of our June departure neared, our friends threw us a bon voyage party. There was a cake. With a lot of imagination, it looked like the Rocky Mountains. That is, if the Rockies are sugarcoated in white and green frosting with pellets of brown sprinkles as roads. On the cake were two tiny, handmade copper bicycles.

One of the patrons took the bikes and gave a puppet show on the cake mountains.

"This is Jan," he said, holding one bike.

"This one is Marty," he said holding the other.

Then, he positioned the bikes on various sweet locations, providing hilarious commentary about the different situations: Jan ahead of Marty, Marty waiting for Jan, Jan on a steep pitch, Marty on a downhill, Jan making sushi, Marty eating ramen noodles again.

After the show, another well-wisher took Jan aside and said, "Just promise me one thing, if something breaks, don't try and fix it. Just get a ride."

That might sound silly, but it did show the concern many friends had about Jan's first big bicycle adventure. They knew her as Jan the mom or Jan the chef or Jan who lives down the street and has a somewhat normal life despite that bicycling boyfriend of hers. Jan was leaving that familiar, safe, pigeonholed existence for something new, risky, and exciting to those who didn't mind sleeping in a tent.

So Jan couldn't promise she would fly home at the first sign of trouble.

But there was one promise - adventure.

We would find it at the border of British Columbia and ride the heavily forested area of northwest Montana to a sliver of Idaho and then the broad basins of Wyoming. We would cross the High Country of Colorado and the deserts of New Mexico, ending in the barren area near the Chihuahua border. On paper, there is 695 miles in Montana, 72 miles in Idaho, 481 miles in Wyoming, 544 miles through Colorado and 678 miles of riding in New Mexico.

Before we left, we agreed on a couple of things. Both of us would carry whistles. No one would make a turn in the road unless both of us were there. We would call our mothers and tell them we were fine. We would stick religiously to the main route not taking any alternative paved routes offered in places that might be impassable during heavy rains. We would accept no rides.

We expected to take about 12 weeks to experience the generosity and maelstroms of nature, humanity and each other.

Together, we would ride the Divide.

Chapter Three

CONTINENTAL DIVIDE
PACIFIC   ATLANTIC

Whitefish, Montana

Tom Petty was right. The waiting is the hardest part.

We were in Whitefish, Montana, aching to bust out on the trail. There was a problem, however.

We were there. All our gear was not.

The great plan to outsmart the snafu gods was simple. Ship the equipment ahead to Whitefish, about 60 miles from the start of the Great Divide. We had a contact there. His name was Chucky, a take-life-as-it-comes television camera guy at Polar Bear Productions. Chucky, a.k.a. Bryan Allen, was the friend of a friend back home named Amy Quigley (now married and named Amy Mahoney) who worked at Resort Sports Network. She called Chucky and asked if he would take care of us during our stay in northern Montana. He would. We could send everything to his office and he would shuttle us in his red pickup truck complete with golden labrador riding shotgun to the start of the ride.

A week before our June 23 Whitefish arrival, we shipped four boxes to Chucky. Two contained the bikes and two held trailers plus assorted equipment we could fit inside them like the tent and sleeping bags.

In theory, sending the gear ahead provided less worry. The plan was to fly from Portland, Maine via Philadelphia to Seattle and then take a 19-hour bus ride to Whitefish. We wouldn't have to lug the bikes and trailers around with us and deal with getting them from the airport to the bus terminal.

The chosen route wasn't exactly direct, but it was cheap and I like cheap. A friend in the airline business got us a rate we couldn't pass up for the Portland-Seattle flight while the bus tickets cost next to nothing.

Not having the worry gave us time to explore Seattle a bit during a 15-hour wait for the bus to Montana. We went to Chinatown in search of bowls of pho at a restaurant. Pho is a delicious noodle soup filled with chunks of meat and fish surrounded by vegetables in a broth. It is fun food. Eat the meat and noodles with chopsticks and slurp the soup with a spoon.

After the pho, it was time for flying fun with food. We made a path to the bustling fish market and its many scents of fish, teas and fruits. We sampled what we could and watched the gravity defying skills of the fish throwers as they hucked pisces from display case to wrapping paper to scale to shopping bag. Salmon jerky caught Jan's eye and we picked up a few pieces. She thought it would go well with some kind of pasta down the road.

Armed with the jerky, we made it to the bus station and got on the bus for the long, uncomfortable ride to Whitefish. Long distance bus travel isn't much fun. The sterile stench of the bathroom is unpleasant. The leg room is never enough. No matter how hard you try - from the fetal position to knees high on the seat back in front of you - there is never a comfortable position. The bait of adventure can make it bearable.

During a stop in Missoula, a few hours south of Whitefish, there was time during a pit stop to make a quick telephone call to Chucky and let him know we were almost there. That's when I learned all our gear hadn't arrive. He said one box had arrived. By his description, it sounded like the package contained a trailer.

That wasn't a problem, I reported back to Jan during the post-telephone call gear update. All packages sent at the same time don't always arrive at the same time was my rationale. It was just a small glitch in the cosmos of travel. Everything would work out. The gear would probably show up in the morning and we would be on our merry way.

Chucky met us at the bus drop-off with his dog, Bubba. The

MARTY BASCH

description he had given of himself was right on: six feet tall and bald. With the one box in the back of his truck, our new friend drove us to a hotel in town where Jan and I would spend the night. We could shower, get horizontal and rest fitfully because in the morning, all our gear would show up.

That didn't happen. Only one box was delivered. It contained the other trailer. So, now we had two trailers and the equipment we had stuffed in them: a tent and two sleeping bags. At worst case, we could rickshaw our way down the Divide.

So began the arduous task of contacting the shipping company, reading them the tracking numbers, and being told the remaining two packages were on their way. Delay costs money. There are more nights in a hotel room, more meals to be eaten at restaurants. Then there is the additional stress. Anxiety starts to slip onto the stage. All of a sudden, it doesn't make sense that if all four boxes were sent at the same time, they should be arriving one by one, day after day. Though we put on our happy faces to Chucky and the colleagues he introduced us to, inside we were simmering and angry at anyone associated with brown parcel trucks.

We tried to whittle away the hours with errands and sightseeing. Chucky was nice enough to take us into Glacier National Park with its snow-covered peaks. A highlight was seeing a black bear cross the road. Bears do roam in Montana and not just black bears, but grizzly bears as well. The Montana papers had headlines about a killer grizzly in the park and locals talked about people getting "munched" by griz.

That reminded us it would be a good idea to pick up a couple of cans of grizzly bear repellant. We hoped they would be more of souvenirs than necessities. The Divide Route cut through griz country and I had no intention of a repeat face-to-face grizzly bear encounter like I had in Alaska in 1994. Alone on a dirt road deep in Denali National Park, a griz and I happened upon one another. As luck would have it, a couple was able to save me from the bear deciding whether he wanted to eat me or not.

Chucky was an able tour guide and led us from the park to a couple of legendary Whitefish haunts at night on the wooden sidewalks of Central Avenue. In the smoke-filled bar, The Palace, and later at the crowded Northern, Jan and I would recount our tale to everyone we were introduced to by Chucky. We were waiting. It was hard. Chucky suggested we move from the hotel to his house. We did. Maybe that would make everything better.

It did, at least for me.

On our third day in Whitefish, the remaining two boxes arrived. They contained the bikes. Both battered, blackened, and bruised boxes looked as though they had already completed the Divide trip. One had a particularly nasty gash.

The sliced box contained Jan's bike. The hole foreshadowed the bad news inside. Not all of her bike had made it.

In packing the bike, we were instructed to remove the pedals. We affixed them to each bike with duct tape. Only one pedal was there. The bike's headset - the parts that hold the front fork together with the handlebar - was missing too. When packing a bike, the handlebar has to be turned parallel to the bike so it can fit into the box. The headset is loosened. Apparently, it wiggled its way out of the box through the hole as well.

Seeing her bike, Jan did not have kind words for the shipping company and let loose a flurry of epithets. At the same time, tears of frustration flowed too. What else could go wrong, she wondered.

There would be plenty more challenges in the coming miles. In the meantime, Chucky loaded us into his truck and drove us to a local bike shop where, in about two hours, Jan's bike was fixed and ready to roll. (The shipping company later reimbursed me for the expenses). Life was finally looking up.

During the drizzle of a June 26 Montana morning, Chucky, Bubba, Jan, and I headed north in the truck from Whitefish to the Canadian border and Port of Roosville, the checkpoint between the two countries. Joy and apprehension took turns rumbling in my stomach. I was happy to get going, ready for the open road and adventure. But, I was also cutting the umbilical cord to familiarity. The whiz of a fast-paced world was about to be replaced by the spin of a pedal.

Our passports were stamped on the Canadian side. Chucky

MARTY BASCH

brought his video camera to record the start of the journey. With a kiss and couple of I love you's, Jan and I took off on what she called "the trip of a lifetime."

Optimism reigned. The drizzle abated. There were smiles. The adventure had begun. We were pedaling the first of thousands of miles. Nothing could stop us now.

After a quarter of a mile, Jan reached over on her handlebar to shift her chain into a higher gear.

"Damn," she yelled under the big sky.

Her chain fell off.

It was a quick fix. In less than a minute, Jan was back in the saddle again. We rode by a field of wildflowers and Jan decided to stop and pick a few. She added a handful to her handlebar bag and gave one to me. She put one in her bicycle helmet. Frustration and bike boxes were now a memory. Chucky and Bubba were on their way back to Whitefish. We were untethered.

The wheels spun through the gold and green flats of Tobacco Valley, framed by dark, brooding mountains under a gray western sky. Horses roamed in the meadows cordoned off by barbed-wire fences. Hay was harvested and rolled up, waiting to be stored. Walkers greeted us with a howdy instead of a hello. A couple of wild turkeys brazenly crept up to our bicycles and followed us in a zany race for maybe one hundred yards. Domestic llamas posed for pictures behind a wooden fence. Songbirds were perched on barbed wire.

We pedaled through the tiny town of Eureka and left the paved backroads for the dirt leading into the timber-heavy Kootenai National Forest, the Flathead National Forest, and Stillwater State Forest. The miles clicked away in the forests. This was to be a short day on the road with a late morning start and then the fatigue that followed the tension of the delayed start.

Worry can be replaced. If yesterday had been worries about bike boxes, today Jan had a new worry - grizzly bears!

As the miles passed, we approached an area described on the map as a "glorious descent through wild country." This was followed by "Watch for grizzly bears."

We did not want to watch for grizzly bears. That implied we would see them. We did not. All we wanted was a safe place to camp by a stream and then fall quickly to sleep.

Jan carried the map. The map was kept in a see-through case on her handlebar bag so it could be easily consulted. This meant those ominous words were in her face constantly.

Also not far from her face was the pepper spray. The nozzles of the spray cans peeked through our handlebar bags as we rode. We were like two outlaws on the dusty streets of a tumbleweed town waiting for a high noon shoot-out.

It was well after noon and we scanned the forest for that ideal campsite. The map suggested places to camp. There was a spot at mile 22. Jan considered 22 miles a wimpy first day. She wanted to do 30 miles the first day out.

The beauty of America's national forests is there are ample opportunities for camping. Though there are scores of developed campsites along the route, those who know where to look can find other equally enchanting spots. If you don't know where to look, it helps to know how to ask.

We stopped to discuss where to camp. Jan wanted to set up camp well outside of the grizzly bear watch range. Who could blame her?

As happenstance would have it, a pickup was heading slowly down the dirt road towards us. As it got closer, I flagged it down.

The woman behind the wheel was a member of the forest work crew. She was an encyclopedia of information. Jan unloaded her worries about griz hanging around and the woman relaxed Jan's fears that a griz was lurking around the next bend for her despite plenty of grizzly bear poop around. The woman suggested a camping spot just off the road. It was on an unmarked path with a picnic table and creek-side real estate.

As rain started to fall, we set up camp and quickly established a routine. We worked as a team, setting up the tent, throwing in the sleeping pads and bags. The overhang of the tent acted as a dry portico where items could be stored. I would get water, start the stove, and make tea. Jan would do the slice and dice routine,

21

creating one pot wonders; this night a little fish jerky from Seattle with ramen noodles.

We retired early that night, with pellets of rain hitting the tent fly. Jan, forever surprising, pulled out two inflatable camping pillows I had no idea she had. She handed them to me and I blew them up. Sleep came quickly. It wasn't even eight o'clock.

Dreams? Who knows. But neither of us thought as the rain fell we'd soon be right back in Whitefish before the sun shone in the big, blue Montana sky again.

SALMON WIGGLE (ramen style)

Ingredients:
2 packages seafood ramen noodles
1 piece, about four to eight ounces, of dried salmon jerky
1 can of peas

Directions:
Boil ramen noodles. The spice package may be saved for another meal because the dried salmon jerky adds enough flavor. Cut the salmon into small pieces and add to cooked noodles. The fish will soften the longer it sits in the pot. Drain peas and add to pot. After you're done eating, wiggle into your sleeping bag and go to sleep.

Chapter Four

CONTINENTAL DIVIDE
PACIFIC   ATLANTIC

Canadian border to Whitefish, Montana
(again)

The first one hundred miles of any bike trip are a reality check. It is a chance to monitor both body and equipment for defects. For three days, northern Montana tested both ourselves and gear in a proving ground of mud and rain as the ride led right back to where we started: Whitefish.

The body is the first to protest being torn away from worldly modern comforts and put to work as a pack mule. A sedentary lifestyle is but a memory. Reality becomes aches and pains as muscles and tendons voice their displeasure of having not been consulted about going on a long distance bike ride. The gluteus, groin, and lower back round out the chorus of moans and groans that can be silenced temporarily with ibuprofen taken with morning tea and oatmeal, and every few hours afterwards.

Perspiration makes an entrance from a few new places on the body. It's not called perspiration anymore. It's sweat. Women sweat. Men sweat. Instead of pouring from foreheads, under armpits, and the chest, sweat creeps from crevasses behind the ears and from the lower back. It is wrung out at day's end from both bike gloves and the pads inside a bicycle helmet. It is, to quote any warm-blooded 10 year-old, gross.

Kinks in gear come alive. The first casualty was Jan's odometer. She knew something wasn't right when she clocked herself at 156 miles per hour on the downside of the Whitefish Divide, the natural border between the Kootenai and Flathead National Forests. This was also a spot, where according to the map, grizzly bears may roam. Jan wanted to be out of there fast, but she's not that quick.

My trailer gave me a scare. It became unattached from the bike without permission and jammed into the rear wheel's spokes, stopping me cold. The result was a bellowing string of profanity that would have frightened away any grizzly bear. Thankfully, the spokes suffered no damage. This was a simple case of not tightening the right part securely enough.

In those three days, flashes of nature were everywhere. At the start of the day, white-tailed deer paraded deeper into the forest when the gravel of the dirt road gave away our approach. Chipmunks and squirrels scampered ahead or stood atop a stump as if to give us a look-over.

Flashes of man were everywhere too. One burly type was cutting wood by the road. Lost in his own thoughts, he was startled when we stopped to ask him about griz. He reassured us of no bears in the area and enlightened us to upcoming water opportunities.

Our imagination saw bear everywhere. One man even first looked like a bear from a distance. If it moved, it was a bear. Yards ahead at the top of a hill, there was movement.

"What do think?," Jan asked. "Bear?"

"Can't tell," I said.

The creature, complete with headband, stood its ground as we gingerly and cautiously pedaled up the hill.

The bear was a bearded, bespectacled man.

We didn't feel all that foolish because after exchanging roadside pleasantries, the man confessed he saw us differently from a distance too.

"Thought you were a bear," he said. The man told us he had seen two grizzly the day before so his bear radar was on high.

People are a great information source while on the road. They also pepper you with questions. Long distance mountain bikers are always magnets for questions. About 30 miles outside of Whitefish, the solitude of Red Meadow Lake with its stunning reflections of snow-stocked mountain ravines was broken when a Minnesota church group in two white vans pulled up to admire the vista too. In no time, the friendly questions, the same ones that would follow us for the duration for the ride, came at us. Where are you from? Where are you going? See any bears? (Okay, this would change later as we moved from bear country to say elk, deer, moose or snake country). How many miles do you go in a day? What do you eat? Where do you sleep? What do you do when it rains? Have any flats?

We answered the questions. We would also encourage them to follow the trip on the web sites. We also gathered a few more e-mail addresses for Jan's weekly newsletter to family and friends.

How your perspective can change while traveling by bicycle. Just a few days before we couldn't wait to get out of Whitefish and now we were on our way back. When we got there, it became a pleasure dome of civilization with indoor accommodations, restaurants, stores, bike shops, and laundrymats.

It even had a car wash which we used to spray off the Montana mud we reluctantly had collected on everything. Spotted-skunk-stripe was the fashion of the trail, streaked up our backs and on the important rain shells. Want to spot Jan? Look for the honeybee in yellow and black. The purple nurple was me - purple and black. Mud caked the chain and gears. Trailside sticks were used to eradicate the thick goo.

Whitefish was a place to regroup, refuel and dry out. Check in with Chucky. Have a beer. Shower. Sleep inside at a hostel. Put the stove away.

We were able to dry everything out while we rested and restocked our supplies.

Going shopping on a bike trip can be lots of fun, even for guys.

You never know what you are going to find. Down on gasoline for the stove, I took the canister to a filling station. There is total joy in standing at a gas pump with canister in hand, filling up a 16 ounce tank while motorists pump away at their gas-guzzling vehicles. There is victory in finishing pumping and seeing that your tab is maybe 18 cents.

I walked into into the store, and picked up a couple of coffees too. Coffees and canister in hands, I sauntered up to the register ready to pay.

The young lady behind the register tallied up everything.

"Eighteen cents, please," she said.

"But what about the two coffees?," I said.

"Oh, they're free with a fill-up," she said.

That story got laughs that night as Jan and I revisited the watering holes of Whitefish with Chucky and his friends. We went over the lessons of the first 100 miles and wondered how it was that the Canadian border was some 60 miles or so from Whitefish and we had put on over 100 miles on our bikes. Clearly, the Great Divide Mountain Bike Route is not the shortest distance between two points. It is the road less traveled, the high road. It weaves, bobs, and snakes its way through alpine meadows, over sharp-edged mountains, and by soothingly clear, cold, lakes and creeks. In the first three days it became apparent that the Great Divide was a long way to nowhere.

Montana is called the "Big Sky" state because of its big, blue skies. So far, the elusive blue sky was painted with clouds. Nature's curtain of low clouds had proved a big tease, only allowing us a few glimpses of the tall pines, rocky ledges and stubborn snow.

On a rest day, we dried out, eliminated most of the mud, stretched our aching muscles and joints, popped a few more pain relief tablets, and purchased a new odometer for Jan.

The weather forecast changed. Wouldn't you know it, it finally looked like there were big, blue skies ahead.

Chapter Five

Whitefish to Condon, Montana

Montana Charlie's wasn't supposed to be there. But this was no mirage. The roadside oasis was as real as the thick cheeseburgers, sweet fried ice cream and frosty cheap beers we stuffed down our collective gullets and into our appreciative stomachs.

One of the best scenarios on any adventure is when the unexpected turns up positive. Unexpected can also be a royal pain in the butt like when it's gear problems, and there was some of that before getting to the woodsy Condon restaurant on stark Route 83.

Inside Montana Charlie's we found the steady gaze of stuffed trophy animal heads on the bar wall. Dead animals are good drinking buddies. They look you straight in the eyes, appear to listen and don't say much.

So inside, they heard Jan and I recount much about the three days and 110 miles between Whitefish and this watering hole, from the unexpected pleasure of being inside a bar to the nagging displeasure of Jan's bike woes.

The rest day in Whitefish gave us renewed zest. Montana's big sky lived up to its name. For the second time, we left Whitefish with Chucky and his lab Bubba. This time, there was a friend Johnny and the three - though Bubba didn't help much - spent about an hour or so videotaping us under the sunny skies.

27

Saying good-bye again, Jan and I were left to ourselves and maps to get us down the Divide. Maps are a constant companion on the Great Divide. They are folded, refolded, refolded again, squished, squashed, pondered over, looked at, cursed at, and smiled upon over the miles. Each one conquered is a trophy. Each one unfolded for the first time is the beginning of an amazing journey.

Sometimes they're wrong.

I make mistakes too. Despite good intentions, I screw up. I've poured over copy, thinking it's mistake-free. Then a reader writes to the newspaper pointing out my now embarrassing faux pas. It comes with the territory.

West of Whitefish, we entered Columbia Falls, following the map's maze of directions. The streets and landmarks didn't seem to fit. We traced the error back to the map. A left should have been a right. Jan, forever proving correct that women will ask for directions when uncertain while men vow to continue on the path to nowhere, went right up to a work crew on the roof of an auto dealer and became enlightened as to the way out of town.

Sharing her newfound insight with me, we easily left Columbia Falls under the sunshine of the last day of June. Glorious is the Swan River Valley with its dusty backroads, ranches, farms, and the majesty of the Swan Mountains. The mountains, off to the east, provide a rich backdrop. Over the miles, the snow-capped Mission Mountains appeared to the west and sandwiched between the two, we were captivated with mouth-wide-open beauty.

Nature's splendor, sunshine, and easy riding helped push us to cycle what would be 46 miles. This was the most Jan had ever pedaled in one day. It was also the first of many soon-to-be-broken personal best days for her.

Not only was Jan kicking butt on the bike, she was also in culinary glory. South of Columbia Falls, we rode by a greenhouse on Mooring Road. Jan steered us to Fisher's Greenhouse for some roadside grocery shopping of the advertised broccoli, cauliflower and peppers. An ebullient Jan was nearly deflated learning it was too early in the season for those vegetables. The tables turned when the woman who said she owned the place learned Jan was a chef. She invited us to peruse the produce still planted in the ground. Pick it ourselves.

Spinach, thyme, rosemary, parsley, and chives were picked and purchased. Over the miles Jan would use them to spice up her one pan concoctions. We got vegetables and the greenhouse owner got information. She was curious about an increase in the number of mountain bikers passing by her business. She wasn't familiar with the Great Divide route so we told her about it. As would happen in the future, we became ambassadors. Take out the map. Show where we had been. Point out where we are. Place the finger on where we were going. We became quite good at it.

Being two-wheeling spokesmen for the Divide was one thing, but handling the heat was another. Jan didn't do heat well. She prefers snow, wood stoves, and fleece. Heat, combined with the aches and pains of riding, made Jan uncomfortable. She also had some self-doubt during the first few days of the ride of completing the entire journey. Heat did that to her. To compound her misery, I was constantly reminding her to drink water. Staying hydrated while riding is a must and Jan didn't take well to the mantra; drink before you're thirsty.

To escape the heat, we were always looking for shade. We scouted out the cool spots while we rode our bikes or when we walked them, like after eating lunch. We found shade in conventional places like under tall trees and sometimes tried to ride in their shadows, but also when we rested at schools, under picnic tables, and inside convenience stores.

When Jan wanted to stop, we would. When she wanted to call it a day, we did, and found a spot to camp outside of Swan River and east of Flathead Lake.

Too tired to break out the stove, we fell asleep after a meal of peanut butter and jelly sandwiches

Though Jan slept well, she awoke in the morning to being nibbled. Her toes were being tickled. Certainly this can be a pleasant way to start the day, especially if I was doing the tickling. I wasn't. It was something outside the tent.

It was Blazer.

Blazer was brown, playful, and was wearing a green collar with a tag that showed she had gotten her shots in Sandpoint, Idaho.

The dog adopted us. Blazer found us the night before as we set up camp in the tall grass. She decided to bed down outside the tent. In the morning, she acted as a canine alarm clock and licked Jan's feet through the tent's front mesh screen.

Dogs are ubiquitous parts of biking adventures. Wherever you go, there they are snarling, barking, chasing, lapping, wagging, and following.

Following is the part I'm not too crazy about. That wasn't the problem with Blazer. Blazer was staying. When we arrived to set up camp after a tiring day, Blazer caught up to us and tried to get us to play. She jumped, lapped us and put her nose everywhere. We were just too tired to show her much attention. We didn't even give her the crust from those PB and J sandwiches.

After getting her feet licked, Jan melted and prepared the dog a Scooby snack. Blazer had peanut butter and jelly for breakfast.

Blazer didn't help much with packing up to hit the dirt roads in the Flathead National Forest. She didn't have much enthusiasm for being the first dog to wag its way down the Divide to Mexico. So after a couple of "go homes" she finally disappeared from our radar.

We were alone again and slogged up the switchbacks of Crane Mountain. Pavement turned to dirt and the low-traffic national forest roads. Maybe five vehicles would pass us in a day sometimes. We could hear the engines rumble long before they passed us. We could see, and taste, the dust kicked up long after they sped past us.

Gravel became two-track. Swaths of green and wildflowers appeared. Dry dirt led to minefields of mud. Like skiers and snowboarders dream of runs in fresh powder, mountain bikers wish for singletrack, narrow ways on hard-packed dirt through the woods. Though pieces of singletrack are scarce on the Divide, they are there. Sometimes well-defined double track, made by engine-powered vehicles over the years, also gives that velvet feel of singletrack.

New landmarks waited for us. Instead of traffic lights, cairns, those rock piles used by hikers, signaled we had come upon a turn. They were made by others who had already pedaled parts of the route. Billboard after billboard was replaced by the brown and white signs in the national forest indicating towns ahead. Loggers tape hanging from trees marked boundaries. Each creek we passed by was as big a landmark to us as driving by a highway rest area on the interstate. Roads didn't have names like Elm, Maple, or Pine, but bore numbers like Forest Road 903 or Forest Road 9591. Every campsite became a place to stop, rest and fill up on water. Forest gates, used to keep unwanted motor vehicles out of the national forest, became routine sightings. Bikers went around them. Cattle guards, used to secure cattle in an area, were easily navigated on bicycle once we felt comfortable going over the narrow slots.

Tall pines gave way to alpine vistas of distant ravines with snow. Mosquitoes stalked us. Bees buzzed. Butterflies fluttered. Daisies lit up meadows. Tall grasses tickled our calves. Deep in the forest, there were times it felt like there was no one else in the world. It was our trail, our ride. There were no cars, no SUVs. This was bliss.

We shared our happiness with other Divide riders because we weren't always by ourselves. Trailside meetings could end up lasting minutes or turn into group rides for a few days. The first fellow rider we met was a guy named Stuart from Kansas. We bumped into him in Whitefish and again on the lush Fatty Creek Road between Swan Lake and Condon. As we took a break, he rode up to us. Not everyone has a summer to ride the Divide. Many riders do sections, and Stuart was riding pieces of it to Colorado. Young and fast, he was soon on his way after bringing us news of a couple of riders behind us.

Sometimes news would come to us by looking up at the sky. Western afternoon thunderstorms were new to us. As the miles clicked by, we would use them as a signal to sometimes stop for the day. That's what happened as we saw the darkening clouds above us as we cycled through the Lolo National Forest. At a junction of a fire road and Wes Morrell Road, we set up camp in

MARTY BASCH

time to weather the fast-moving storm. We clung to each other as
the storm blew through, making the earth shake, our tent flutter,
and Jan wondering what the hell she was doing in Montana in the
first place.

The next day brought us to Montana Charlie's after hours
of obstacles beginning with a grueling two mile push over a hill
followed by searing
heat even in the dark
and deep forest with
its hidden streams
and creeks running
within earshot.

Summer travelers
traversing the
nation's roads by
motorized vehicles
have to contend
with construction
and alternate routes.
It's no different on
the Divide. A sign
warned us of a closed
road ahead. But to
whom was it closed?
Was it the motorized
crowd or mountain
bikers? We decided it was the former since we didn't see any signs
for an alternate route.

Fisher's Florentine Pasta
Ingredients:
1 pound of pasta
1 bag spinach or a batch of garden picked
spinach
2 bullion cubes
1 tablespoon dehydrated onion flakes
1 tablespoon dehydrated garlic flakes
grated parmesan, optional

Directions:
Pull stems from spinach and discard.
Break spinach into pieces, wash, drain, set
aside. Boil enough water to cook pasta,
drain and set aside. Place instant onion
and garlic flakes in enough water to
reconstitute. Heat and add bullion cubes.
When simmering add the spinach. As
you stir, it will shrink. Toss in pasta. If
desired, top with grated parmesan.

The closed road was gated and had been blocked with huge
boulders. We could go around. But first we needed to detach the
trailers and carry them over and through the boulders. Then we had
to lug the bikes through the boulders, at times a tight squeeze.

After that, bad luck followed Jan.

The road deteriorated as we progressed with sand, mud, bumps,
and ruts. Jan's progress was hampered even more by a problem
shifting her gears. She preferred lower gears that made it easier for

32

her to pedal and tried without success to get her chain to the correct chain ring. The bike parts balked and clinked while she grunted and swore.

Further insults came in the form of blowdowns, trees that had been toppled by nature and left across the trail. We became sherpas again, lugging bike and trailer over the downed trees. Maybe it was when we carried her bike over one of the trees, or when we had to squeeze through the boulders, but Jan's derailleur was bent and shifting became troublesome.

A light breeze tried to cool things down, but Jan was too caught up in misery to see the glory of the picturesque mountains around us. Stopping at a creek to rest, filter water, and get a better handle on the problem didn't help much either. The derailleur could be bent back, but might there be consequences? We opted to wait a bit and see if we could find a bike shop once we got back to paved Route 83, outside the town of Condon.

The first car Jan saw, she flagged down. Pelted with a refreshing blast of air-conditioning as the car's window came down, Jan asked the people inside if there was a bike shop in the area. They didn't know. But they did offer the use of their car phone. But she turned it down and the car continued down the road.

"Who would I call?," Jan would later ask over a beer.

Jan wasn't the only one running with trouble. After the car sped away, I turned around and encountered a dust devil, a twist of wind coming right at me. Jan's pain turned to complete and total laughter as the small twister came for me. Like a deer caught in the headlights, I was frozen. What should I do? Run away, I decided.

In an instant, I leaped from my bike and made a beeline out of its path. The devil went right over the bike, doing absolutely nothing. My gear was scattered not because of the dust devil, but because I had dropped it. Jan's laugh became tears and if I had a tail, it would have been firmly secured between my legs.

Jan's bike was wounded. My pride took a hit, and there up the road was Montana Charlie's. It wasn't listed on our map since it was built after the map was printed.

MARTY BASCH

In the bar, we would figure out what to do. Stools, video gambling, jukebox, and a billiard table were on the inside with the stuffed animal heads on the wall. We could camp for five bucks behind the restaurant, though the bartender tried to convince us the campground down the road at Holland Lake was nicer. We explained we had found our oasis.

Decisions. What to do about Jan's bent derailleur? We could call an 800 number and have a new one delivered. We could call ahead to Seeley Lake, population 870, and see what bike parts they had at the sporting goods store. We could wait for a passing bicyclist with a pocket tool and some bike repair experience to pass by Montana Charlie's and bend it back in shape.

Glad we chose the latter.

Chapter Six

Condon to Seeley Lake, Montana

The parade wasn't for Jan, but it should have been. She deserved to ride high on a float comprised of a huge plastic cow, wave to the crowd, and toss candy out to the kids scampering into the street.

Any mountain biker who survives the blowdowns and other trail demons by Grizzly Basin might feel like the town of Seeley Lake is coming out en masse to throw them a parade.

The parade was at 2 p.m. and we were unknowingly right on time. It was the Fourth of July and while Americans were firing up the backyard grills for a noontime picnic, chilling the beers, and snagging another handful of fat-filled potato chips from big plastic bowls, Jan was having another crappy morning.

This should not have come as a surprise. Just the name Grizzly Basin was a hint of what may be ahead: grizzly bear. That put the nerve meter on high even before she left the tent.

The route to the Basin included a tough hill climb of nearly six miles followed by a four mile section of rocks, blowdowns and washouts all along the northeast shoulder of Richmond Peak.

Up before the mosquitoes in the morning chill, the game plan was to be on the road by 6:30 a.m. and use the early shade and cool temperatures to beat the heat in the pine-heavy Lolo National

Forest. Low-lying clouds initially cloaked the alpine scenery and rains from the night before soaked the ground before the sun worked its magic on the clouds and dirt roads.

Instead of riding, we were pushing our bikes up the Richmond Peak switchbacks, over 7,000 feet high. Jan's breath came in syncopated spurts.

"Marty....wait.....water....rest."

So the routine began. Push a little, rest a little. Drink some water. Reach into the handlebar bag, take out some candy, and pop it down the hatch. Life slowed to a hiker's pace of two miles per hour.

In an attempt to crack a smile on her face, I dug into my arsenal of self-deprecating humor. I reminded her of last night. Two thunderstorms ripped through the area where we had made camp. During the second one, we fell asleep. Upon awakening, I was ready to start what I thought was a new day after a fitful night of sleep.

Jan took a good look outside the tent.

"I didn't know the sun rose in the west," she said.

Turns out we hadn't slept the night, but just an hour or so.

The anecdote did get a laugh, but it was short-lived. The road didn't smooth out fast enough and we slogged up the mountain.

Jan's nerves were being tested. She was scared. Grizzly Basin was not the place she wanted to be spending the holiday. She would look down from time to time and see reminders that bear did call the Basin home. There was scat, but we never did see a bear that day.

We huffed it above the clouds, the mist enshrouding the valley below. It was like a day at the beach, but without water. The clouds, like the tide, crept up to the tall pines and created a line in the alpine valley which didn't seem to move much.

As nature's curtain slowly parted, we saw the now familiar Swan and Mission Mountains. The Swans, to the east, had rich green slopes, like carpet. The Missions, far away to the west, were blackened, featureless masses draped in snow.

Like the map promised, the route deteriorated to brittle red rock amidst the beauty. Sweet singletrack to the fat tire fiend, it was not welcomed by Jan. The track followed the edge of a cliff. Jan-sized evergreens grew in the path, playing a sinister game of slap and tickle as the branches tried to knock us off our bikes.

We crossed over at least six blowdowns as we descended toward Seeley Lake. With the gear, it was a grunt. We carried our stuff over some downed trees. Others, lying in all sorts of strange positions, we nearly had to crawl under.

Not soon enough for Jan, the route improved and the singletrack eventually widened and turned into a two-track delight. Jan's hollers of joy echoed through the valley as the road turned to a normal dirt road the closer we got to Seeley Lake.

The small town was preparing for its afternoon parade. Last minute alterations were being made to the floats as we rode down the main street in search of a campground. We had only completed 22 miles, but you don't pass up a parade while on a bike trip. In the middle of the resort town (home to miles of cross-country ski trails and snowmobile routes), we found a campground which overlooked the fire hall and small lakeside homes. We figured we wouldn't get much sleep that night since the hall was buzzing with activity.

After we set up camp, we headed for the parade. Horses pulled covered wagons. Antique cars draped with American flags rolled slowly down the route. People lined the street, sitting in lawn chairs, standing, or using pickup truck tailgates.

We bought tacos at a stand to help the school's Spanish Club with their trip to Mexico. I took a few swings with an ax and a mallet on a demolished truck as part of a fundraiser for the golf team. We ended up down by the fire hall, passing children participating in a relay race, to pig out on the pig roast.

During our walk, we met a couple of fellow New Hampshire cyclists - Jim and Dale Blodgett - riding the Divide as well. They were engineers, and Jim carried a solar-powered Global Positioning System on his handlebars. As the trip progressed, we would exchange e-mail (they went to libraries for computers) with them. They gave us an idea of what was ahead.

They also convinced us to change our way of carrying things. Our mantra was "you want it, you carry it." But they suggested the stronger rider should carry the most weight. That meant me. Jan liked the idea immediately. So we decided to do a little arranging before we left town. I never noticed a difference while Jan enjoyed hauling less gear.

That evening, while chowing down with the locals during the fire hall pig roast, the day's misery seemed like it had been years ago. We talked about the trip with people seated by us in front of the long wooden table. We met other Seeley Lake visitors too, traveling by RV, heading across the country.

This was Independence Day. It was all about the red, white, and blue. We were red from exposure to the sun and nasty, itchy insect bites. Our unexposed skin was still pure white and in terms of blue, we had a few black and blue marks from being bumped up a bit.

Jan had her independence day too. She had conquered Grizzly Basin and Richmond Peak. It was a time to celebrate, not just the birth of our country - and what a way to see it - but we had just completed 245 miles of the route, the whole first page of the first map.

Chapter Seven

Seeley Lake to Helena, Montana

Sixty miles separates Seeley Lake from Lincoln, a town linked to a modern day criminal, and it took us two days to ride it.

The way was mostly on dirt roads which gave us a chance to see wildlife, mostly deer. Being early risers, we would often hit the road when deer were going out for breakfast. They would stand alert, sense our presence and bolt, too quick for the camera but offering snapshots of wildlife cast in the glow of an early morning light.

We pedaled through the Blackfoot Valley. Though ripe with rippling mountains, ranches and horses, the landscape was changing. It didn't look as lush as the forests we encountered in the first 200 miles. The further south and east the Route went, the less dense the forests appeared. There was beauty in the open sky, tall grasses and colorful wildflowers.

About the only sign of civilization before Lincoln was Ovando, a blip on paved Route 200. To escape the noon heat, we stopped in Trixie's Saloon, furnished with wooden stools, stuffed heads, pool table, Keno, beer, and burgers.

It was time to stoke our furnaces. Appetites change dramatically on extended physical voyagers. Jan, who doesn't have much of a taste for soda, started to develop one because it was readily available and more importantly, cold. She also had a habit of not finishing all of her meal. Now she would.

As for me, if I see it, I eat it. I'd order a burger and fries, and for dessert, I'd order a burger and fries.

Jan's beer consumption improved as well. At the end of the day, she'd have one. For lunch? That was a bit too early. But at Trixie's, with it so hot, she needed to cool off and relax. So she ordered a beer.

She was quick to discover that biking, heat and beer don't mix. Before we mounted our bikes, Jan decided she needed a nap. Right outside the saloon, under some shade, Jan snoozed. Customers walked in and out as Jan slept. Afterward, she was rested, but it was the first and last time she had a beer while cycling.

Outside Ovando, the road turned super flat. Cattle, mules and horses watched us pass by. At times, they would stand in the road, parting when we got within their comfort zone.

Onward we pedaled through Montana. On the dusty and wide back roads, we would often see dilapidated and weathered cabins. There was one cabin we were searching for even though we knew it wasn't there.

We reached Lincoln, a small town with maybe 530 people, though its most famous resident no longer resides there.

People in town must be asked about him all the time, like the waitress we had in a restaurant.

Handing over a twenty, she answered the question before I even finished it.

"No, I didn't know him. He lived about three and a half miles up Stemple Pass. The cabin isn't there anymore. They took it to Sacramento. There isn't anything there anymore," she said.

Nonetheless, we headed up Stemple Pass Road, which is part of the Route. The road changed from pavement to gravel and wound up through the hills passing the telephone company, local newspaper, county sheriff's office, cattle and horses.

Did he cycle this road? Did he wave to those horses? Did he smile going by the law?

We'll never know.

But at the three and a half mile mark, we stopped. There wasn't much but forest and a few homes nearby.

This was where Ted Kaczynski, the Unabomber, and cyclist once lived. Instead of living under the big sky, the man who pleaded guilty to being the mastermind behind a series of bombings that killed three people and injured 23 between 1978 and 1995, was behind bars. Kaczynski's former home was carried away by the feds.

But Stemple Pass Road was still there and leads to the first of the 29 crossings of the Continental Divide we would record.

Several miles past Ted's place was a forest road which rose steeply along the South Fork of Poorman Creek. On the map, a suggestion was given for an alternate route which alleviates the pain and suffering along this forest road. As Jan and I swore upon an imaginary stack of flat tires not to even think about deviating from the main route, we were soon walking up the sadistic road. We were tired and wanted to camp. There wasn't much space by the side of the road to set up camp, but we found spot a short walk from a stream and decided to make do.

The tent was soon up and the water simmering on the one-burner stove when a pickup truck stopped. Jan happened to be changing out from her bicycling clothes and did a quick switch out of sight, using the tent as a curtain. After she was done, we approached the truck and peeked inside. There was a man and woman. The window rolled down.

"You from Montana?," the man asked after we had chatted a bit.

"New Hampshire," I replied.

"I want to tell you something about Montana," he said.

I thought I knew where this conversation was heading so I interrupted.

"We know about the grizzly bears and mountain lions. We're each carrying pepper spray," I said with a bit of a cocky attitude.

"Landowners," he said.

"You own this land?," I gulped.

"We do."

41

In the nicest possible way, we were told we were trespassing.

The couple in the truck, Larry and Sue, told us of a campsite, off their land, about 1,000 feet up the steep, 4WD road. They invited us to take a look. Jan squeezed into the back of the pickup loaded with groceries from the couples' monthly shopping expedition, and they took off. While they were gone, I started to break down camp.

A half later, everyone was back. Jan had made new friends and Larry and Sue told us to throw our gear into the truck. We pedaled the half mile to the campsite, flat spots by a creek and only a quarter mile from the site of a fatal plane crash which had taken place about three weeks before we arrived.

Next thing you know, Larry and Sue invite us into their octagon-shaped home for dinner! Before the meal, Larry gave us a tour. A contractor, he built the house which is off the grid. The electricity was produced by the flowing creek waters.

What made this whole experience so mind boggling is that we were in Unabomber country. Before moving into prison, the Unabomber lived a few miles from Larry and Sue's.

No, they didn't know him.

Though Lincoln may always be connected to the Unabomber, we'll always think of it as the place we trespassed our way to dinner.

•••

You always remember your first. The day after trespassing our way to dinner, it was time for the first Divide crossing. After 12 days and 322 miles, we would reach the first one.

Each one would be a triumph, a memory, a snapshot of pain, punishment, love, and wherewithal.

First we had to get there but water was in the way.

Water is a topic of conversation on the Divide. Bottled water? You bet. But you're the bottling plant, first filtering and then filling. Water was bountiful in lush, green and wild Montana. There was plenty of the life-giving fluid to drink, cook with, and bathe in.

There was also lots of water to cross.

Five creek crossings stood in the way before the first Divide. There were no bridges. At each crossing, we wondered how deep was the water? Will we sink? Will our gear get soaked?

Boots and socks did get soaked, but with each crossing we gained confidence and skill at navigating them. That was the hidden beauty of the ride. Problems would present themselves and we would have to solve them. As we did this, we were learning more about ourselves and increasing our skill levels on the bike. The same thing happened with cattle guards. Living in the East, we hadn't seen any before coming to Montana. Initially, we feared crossing them, thinking we would slip between the metal bars and break our legs. Now we were pros.

We were also in the land of griz again. Scat was on the trail. The night before Larry mentioned there were probably at least three in the area.

He was right. Beside some scat, we saw footprints. The claws and the pad of the foot were easily visible. Our bear spray was visible too, sticking out of the handlebar bags.

The footprints provided us with a tremendous desire to be anywhere but here among the evergreens, clear-cuts and ramshackle cabins.

Clear-cuts are as common on the Divide as free camping. The scars of harvesting are smack on center stage. Gnarly blackened stumps up close, clear-cuts can also look like shorn sheep from a distance. Whether it is viewed as a blight on the land or wise use of resources is up to the rider. I like paper. I'm a writer. I like the feel of books, magazines, and even the hard copy of a web site story download. Toilet paper is wonderful. Paper towels, cardboard, picnic tables, homes, decks, and the smell of a warming campfire are all because of wood. The downed trees will grow back and provide habitat for wildlife.

But, it's a damn eyesore.

Thankfully, the poor forest road switched to a better maintained road and the trees started to disappear to allow for valley views. The road flattened a bit. We heard cattle in the distance and passed a wooden fence before a junction. The rule was, no one turns without the other.

Except Jan didn't want to turn. According to the map, the Divide was around here somewhere. We couldn't find it. In my mind, each Divide should be marked with an air-conditioned bar that serves frosty beer (soda for Jan) and thick burgers.

At least there should be a sign.

So where was it? A sign would be a no-brainer. It would say Continental Divide and maybe have the elevation. But there wasn't one.

There was nothing obvious. But Jan started to trace our path and wouldn't you know it, by a wooden fence, up in a tree, was a small wooden sign with CD blazed on it.

Her smile was wider than Montana's big sky. What would come to be a tradition at each crossing, we would hug, kiss and butt helmets. Take the obligatory picture. Do the high five thing. Whoop it up for the cattle. Moon the horses. Do any stupid or crazy thing in celebration. The crossings were Divide landmarks. Collect them all and win bragging rights.

We just bagged our first one.

What goes up must come down. That is the adage and most times it is true. Down is a glorious feeling. The miles click by rapidly. The wind cools off the body and whistles through the helmet. It is the big reward, pay back for a job well-done.

Down the winding and dusty road we cycled. It wasn't even 10:30 a.m. and one Divide was in the bag. Jubilation is cycling down by the farms, wildflowers, and fences of Marsh Creek Canyon with the person you love enjoying the same sensation.

Alarm is hearing her scream in pain.

Going maybe 20 miles per hour down the sandy road, Jan slid around a corner, lost control, and flew off her bike. She went left. The bike went right. Flying over her handlebars, she landed with a cry.

Adrenaline took over for both of us in the blur of the accident. Jan was able to get up under her own power, trying to remain calm despite the left side of her body feeling as if it was on fire. She would later describe her fall as "sliding into home plate." Jan was bloodied. Blood ran from the crook of her elbow which had strips of flesh hanging as if they they had been cut. Her shoulder burned. Her thigh was bruised and when she lifted her cycling shorts, there was a maze of blood and black and blue.

Using the first aid kit, we went into action. An antiseptic cloth was used to wash the dirt and sand from Jan's wounds. Toilet paper helped get rid of the blood. We were soon out of band aids and gauze pads. The bruises looked nasty. Might stitches be needed for those hanging strips of flesh? Would the injury be infected? We were in the middle of nowhere and all we had was that first aid kit.

Jan kept her best poker face during the ordeal. Advil helped ease the pain.

Not one car passed during the whole time, no more than a half hour. The accident brought out the stark realization of how alone you are on the Divide, how far away the conveniences taken for granted really are. What is carried in a first aid kit and in each person's bank of experience is what gets you through the bad times.

Jan was banged up but her bike and trailer had come through the accident unscathed. She walked around, smarting from the injuries and made sure every part of body and bike were in working order. As a pins and needles sensation worked through her body, she reached down inside for her reserve of confidence. She would ride on. But we wouldn't tell anyone about this until later on in the trip, after the wounds had healed and more miles had been ridden. There was no point in worrying family. They were sure to have enough concern anyway. Time would move on and the fall would become another tale spun by a trail warrior.

Battered and stiff, Jan gingerly returned to her bicycle to pedal through the remote valley of deserted farms and wide open fields that anesthetized her pain somewhat. The road followed a snaking creek with hills in the distance.

Maybe an hour later the first car of the day happened by. We decided to try to flag it down. Maybe the person inside could give us a quick read on Jan's injuries and perhaps restock some of the supplies we had used. You never know who is going to be inside. Jan's dressings would have to be changed and it looked like we were at least 40 miles and another day away from the the nearest town, which happened to be the state capital of Helena, a city of over 24,000.

If you've just taken a nasty spill, having a Montana highway patrol officer drive by is a good thing. That's exactly what happened. The officer was most helpful, taking a quick look at Jan's wounds and deeming them not too bad. He also gave us a compression bandage, tape and towelette.

We pressed on. With a wounded Jan, Helena now became the carrot and we had to reach it now. We would find a pharmacy and at least have a druggist take a look at Jan. He, like the police officer, was to deem it not so bad. It was worse than it looked.

First we had to get over another hill, the second Divide of the day.

Despite the soreness, the second Divide crossing came and went. Not as spectacular or memorable as the first, there wasn't even a sign this time, no matter how hard we looked. There was a solitary post at crossroads which we took to be the marker. It was there we celebrated and rode downhill, Jan a bit more carefully than the last time.

The Helena National Forest provided a unique camping spot that night, among a grazing band of cattle. The cattle provided moos throughout the evening and made us mindful of where we would step. But that night, Jan was able to sleep fitfully despite the concert and began to heal from the fall that gave her a battle scar on her left elbow which she wears for the rest of her life.

Chapter Eight

Helena to Fleecer Mountain, Montana

The mercury neared the 100 degree mark. According to the locals, we in the midst of an "unusually hot July."

When it's that hot, and shade proves elusive, the last place you want to be riding is up Fleecer Mountain.

It's not that we weren't prepared for Fleecer. We had already been tortured on the rough root ride of Lava Mountain between Helena and Butte. We managed to get past a spooky tunnel outside the one-horse town of Basin. We didn't flinch much as we rode the smooth shoulder of the interstate outside Butte.

We knew the Route would toy with us. Now it was throwing us at Fleecer.

Fleecer, pretty from afar with its rivulets of snow and bald head, sits west of the the mining city of Butte in southwest Montana. At 9,436 feet high, nothing comes close to it in the East. By western standards, that's a pretty nice sized hill. By mountain biking standards, it's pain.

You don't actually crest the summit of this rock, but ride up a flank topping out at over 7,000 feet. Ride, though, isn't the word.

Walk this way is more like it.

This is a place that is forbidding to four wheel drive vehicles. For the insane mountain biker, it is beyond steep. This is a wall, a vertical mound of grass that attracts the elk in winter. In summer, blind followers of the Great Divide Mountain Bike Route are led by their gurus to slaughter.

You don't actually ride Fleecer Mountain, you survive it. You push up its front face through a seductive meadow and then burn your wrists on the way down by pumping brakes, leaning back, walking your bike down the wall's other side, and trying not to get snagged in the sage should you sway from the path. Not only may the sage grab you, but the footing is uncertain through the cleaved soil, pockmarked by the hooves of cattle looking to see if the grass is greener on the other side. Should you ride, initially there is bliss, even a dipsy doodle or two, but the path gets steep quickly. One slip and your nuts hit the handlebar and it's off to the sperm bank for a withdrawal.

The alpine meadow houses real beauty. We were pushing our rigs up through the grassy swatch and saw three deer near the crest. It wasn't a mirage as Mother Nature had the outdoor furnace cranking. Deer, white tails and mule, are quite common in these parts. You can spot them up high and see them stand still, sometimes feeding. Once they get wind of you (which is pretty easy after three or four days with no shower), they freeze. Then, like they've been pierced with a hot needle, they leap across the land, tail dancing in the distance as they seek cover in the forest.

The push up wasn't so bad. We gazed around the valley, drinking in the scenery. But it was downtown time. First, it was smiles.

Then, it was swears.

The path was so steep we couldn't see the bottom. Riding was out of the question. Any wildlife in the area was scared away by the obnoxious sounds of squeaking breaks.

We were going a mile an hour. At times, we would zigzag through the sage. We took a beating, but made it down and eventually were rewarded with a long decent into Wise River.

A few weeks before, a town like Wise River would have been a blip to me. That's when I was in a car. This time, it was an oasis, with a grocery store, and two restaurants.

Jan chose the H-J, up on the hill. It was 88 degrees in the shade when we went in for burgers and a milkshake. We must have looked haggard as we strolled in, all eyes in the small joint on us as we slid into a booth.

We were dog tired, smelly and darkened by the sun, but a man in the neighboring booth struck us up for conversation. Next thing you know, he's inviting us to spend the night at his ranch eight miles down the road.

Getting invited to a stranger's house is always an interesting experience. I have found that many people who invite bikers back to their home usually have a house high atop a hill. Or, sometimes they live just a few miles off the beaten path. Then usually it's up a hill.

But this guy, a pleasant fellow, lived smack off the road we were about to travel down. There were no complicated directions and no unsigned roads to keep an eye on. Most importantly, no big hill stood in our way.

"Sure," I said to the mustached man named Scott wearing a baseball cap. I got directions to his place.

He went back to talking with the two people he was seated with at the booth.

Then came the kick.

Jan whacked me in the shin under the table. Okay, she tapped me a little.

In a moment, before she even said a word, I knew I had done wrong. I had broken a cardinal rule of couplehood: thou must consult thy partner.

The look came first, that steely gaze that curls any puppy's tail. Then came the words.

"Ask him how much it is going to cost."

Jan was new to this bike trip thing. Even after trespassing our way to dinner a few miles ago, she still didn't get it that there are nice people out there who just want to help, or give back, or whatever their reasons happen to be.

"You want me to what?," I said.

"Ask him how much," she answered.

49

It wasn't enough that Fleecer had almost done me in. She had me in a vise and was beginning to squeeze.

Hospitality, it was explained to her, is just hospitality.

The vise squeezed a little more as Scott got up to leave and stopped by the booth to find out when to expect us.

Shifting, squirming and feeling that squeeze, I succumbed to the powerful pressure from the pint-sized iron-fisted ruler of the Divide.

"Um, uh, how much is it going to cost?," I asked.

He seemed somewhat taken aback by this.

"You think I'm going to charge you?," he countered.

Instead of answering, I just gave him the finger, pointing my index finger straight at Jan.

"She does," I said.

He shifted his eyes, looking at Jan.

"It's the best price. It's free," he said.

This seemed to put Jan at ease and she agreed we would be staying at the ranch that night. Scott headed out to go home and soon enough we were back on the bikes easing down the road.

Jan had to be reminded about the kindness of strangers. Just a few nights before we had decided to camp by a few fire rings we saw. There happened to be a couple of guys there splitting wood. Jan walked over to them and asked if we could camp there. They didn't seem to care. Next thing you know, everyone is on a first name basis, we're pouring over the map, then they get out the beer and before taking off, they drop some firewood off to us.

Eight miles later outside the H-J we were in our own cabin on a 200 acre ranch. The comfy rustic cabin with two beds, table, dresser, green carpeting, rocking chair, and welcoming shower looked upon a grassy meadow where in June herds of elk came to feed. Horses grazed in the meadow just beyond the stables.

The main house, at least the room we saw, was immaculate with an elk head over the fireplace and elk horn chandeliers hanging from the ornate wooden ceiling.

That night, we met the ranch hand and some other guests. We had dinner with them. We enjoyed their company.

And afterwards, we fell asleep with sweet dreams of Montana hospitality.

Chapter Nine

Fleecer Mountain to Bannack, Montana

Bannack was born in the intensely hot summer of 1862 when placer gold was discovered in the waters of Grasshopper Creek. Strike gold and they will come. So they did and within a year the southwestern Montana Territory (Montana wasn't a state yet) had a population of 3,000.

As quickly as it went boom, Bannack went bust when another gold strike 70 miles away attracted much of the population.

Now, Bannack stands as an empty ghost town.

From its' wooden sidewalks, it's easy to dream about the Wild West when outlaws hung from gallows high in the hills, the telegraph sent speedy messages and spirits flowed in the rowdy saloon.

Once a year, Bannack lives again. Cowboys and cowgirls mosey down the streets. The stagecoach rolls. Muskets are fired. The blacksmith gets shoes ready for the horses while the Meade Hotel hosts debates about women's suffrage and music plays on its shaded front porch.

Jan and I wanted to see a ghost town during our ride through the West. We just didn't figure to see many people in one.

Bannack was booming again before our very eyes.

Those very same eyes had seen a lot before rolling into

Bannack, a 50 mile ride from the comforts of the post Fleecer Mountain cabin.

We left our generous hosts and pedaled down the road. It was not even 11 a.m., and an old blue Volvo crept by, going maybe 20 or 30 miles per hour. He went to pass us and gave us such a berth, he briefly went off the road on the other side.

Then he returned to the right side of the road and drove out of sight.

But he came back about 10 minutes later. We were resting, perched on a rock. In the distance, we saw the Volvo return, weaving for us.

Nearing us, he stopped, and inched his face out from the open window.

"Youseeenmycamp?" he slurred from the driver seat.

I just shrugged, raising both palms upward.

He shook his head in the negative.

"I can't find my camp," he said.

I just shrugged again.

He started to laugh.

"Can't find it, you seen it," he said, looking at Jan.

"No, haven't seen it," she said.

"Youokay," he asked.

"Yeah," we answered in unison.

He laughed, waved and weaved off, searching for the elusive camp.

Nothing like Bud for breakfast.

That was only one of the oddities, vagaries and wonderment cyclists sometimes find just by minding their own business, letting the wheels spin. A few days before we had met a lone female cyclist who had been on the road for 15 months, touring America, Europe, and Mexico. That was an achievement, but she had a piece of gear with her that was amazing: a bucket. She carried the bucket on the back of her bike and used it as a table, chair and bike stand. She also did her laundry with it, the motion of cycling acting as the spin cycle.

There were also the natural wonders. A moose crashed through some scrub by a creek. Up the crest of a hill, a deer crossed the road. Wildflowers grew in the meadows. The occasional brush with people came in the form of howdies and waves.

To keep down the dust from dirt roads, road crews usually spray down a solvent. This turns the road to mud. If you are behind a working crew, it usually means that you too will become mud. Legs, arms, hair, face, bike, gear all become caked with the crap. Just let it bake, cake and flake or stop in to a small grocery store and use the bathroom to expedite the cleansing process.

Summer cyclists will also experience construction. It is a given like air, water, and invisible insects always finding their way into your head via the ears, nose or mouth. But being on a predominantly dirt route all the way from Canada to Mexico, the last place we thought we would run into the butt crack crowd would be on a dirt road.

That's exactly what happened.

It was by Polaris, a Montana one horse town if there ever was one, with an old bar, a house or two, and a post office over there. Civilization was creeping its way to the one room school house.

The road was being paved.

We found our way from Polaris to Bannack State Park, east of Dillon, and south of the beauty of the Pioneer Mountains.

When we got there, we found humanity in the form of RVers. We had no idea it was a big weekend in the park. This was to be our lucky day. Not that the place wasn't packed and finding a campsite was a chore. It was that this was the weekend for Bannack Days, when the ghost town lives again.

We came across all sorts of people like Jeremy Puckett, an intern for Montana Fish, Wildlife and Parks who let us camp by his tent.

Then there was Harry, or maybe his name was Henry, who was one of the RVers. All you've got to do is say hello and next thing you know it's story time. At 17, this guy decided he wasn't going to have kids. At that time, he also set a goal to retire at 50. So, at 49 and childless, Harry, or maybe it was Henry, decided to hit the road and that is where he had been for 26 years. His plan that summer was to drive up to the Yukon in his rig, a Mitsubishi 4WD which he raved about, to take part in the territory's 100th birthday celebration. His way to take part was to use the raft and motor he carried to ferry his way up rivers and then raft down.

Good old Harry.

Or, was it Henry?

The park was also the place we met some fellow cyclists who we would meet many times over the coming miles. They were a group of teenage girls aged 15 to 17 who were also cycling the Great Divide. They had a trip leader, a support van, and a film crew to record their travels from time to time. They were from a Massachusetts school and one rider was from the town of Wolfeboro, about 30 miles south of our home. There was that New Hampshire connection again.

That night we made new friends with them, Jeremy drove us into Dillon for supplies, and we all tried to fall asleep to the roar of the generator, the banging of buckets, and the roar of a chain saw.

Perhaps that's why Jan and I were up early the next day to start the day walking the wooden sidewalks of Bannack, deserted in the wee hours of the morning save for a lone rabbit.

Eventually, we ate in the once stately Meade Hotel. Located on the main street, the sourdough hot cakes, scrambled eggs and sausage were served up by people in period dress. Once a courthouse, time had peeled the walls and floors of the hotel. Still, it's easy to imagine what once was as we sipped our coffee. After the miles on the road, we knew about the dust these miners must have eaten. To sit at a table with syrup and butter was welcome relief from squatting on a camping pad which covered the patties left by the cattle that went moo in the meadows.

After breakfast, we came across a culinary item that caught our eyes - Rocky Mountain Oysters. Hailing from the East, oysters reminded us of the distant ocean and hardworking fishermen. This would be a unique lunch.

These oysters were different. To catch them, it's best to have a strong rope and sharp knife. The oysters, looking like miniature hot dogs or rubber bullets, are deep fried and served with either Ranch dressing or cocktail sauce. Advertised as "a nickel a nut," I quickly handed over my dollar for 20 of the rubbery morsels.

I watched as 20 oysters were taken from buckets with metal tongs, dredged in batter and placed in the sizzling oil. In what seemed like a minute, they were being lifted by the tongs again, a brown coat on the little things.

The oysters, now on the plate, sat near both dipping sauces. I dipped left. I dipped right. There was just a burst of flavor from the meat.

Rocky Mountain Oysters are calf testicles. When the calves are branded by ranchers they are also castrated. A delicacy? I'm not so sure. It's more of a passage I think.

That night, we were back by the tent. Jan, who felt a bit sorry for those poor calves but acknowledged their fate, came up with a recipe for using a different part of the cow in a burrito. Of course, you can wrap anything in a burrito, but I had my fill of Rocky Mountain Oysters.

BANNACK BURRITOS

Ingredients:
1 pound hamburger
1 jar of salsa
1 can of refried beans
2 tomatoes
1 onion
lettuce
1 package of pepper jack cheese
1 package of flour tortillas
2 tablespoons cumin

Directions:
Dice the onion and tomatoes, chop the lettuce and cube the cheese. Sauté hamburger. Add enough salsa to cover meat. Stir in the cumin. Start building your burrito. Place the lettuce, cold refried beans, tomatoes, onions, cheese, and meat mixture on top of tortilla. Fold bottom up and roll in the sides. We found by combining all the leftover ingredients (burrito hash), it was even better the second day.

Chapter Ten

Bannack to the Tetons in Wyoming via Idaho

After what seemed like eons, we finally left Montana - 696 miles behind us. On our last night in the state, we sat down for that backcountry dinner theater with fence-jumping cattle in the Centennial Valley after more than three weeks away from home.

But Montana did have to show us one more time who is boss. The last push was up the Continental Divide and Red Rock Pass at 7,120 feet. As if on cue, a transplanted Vermonter in a white Cadillac showed up and took the mandatory photos at the sign as we crossed into our second state - Idaho.

On paper, the spud state was to be 73 miles of relatively flat terrain. Paper can be deceiving. It was flat, but that didn't make it fun all the time.

The road initially took us to Henry's Lake, where anglers hooked 10-pound plus trout. Back among the pine forest and the patches of shade, the Targhee National Forest was home to a few moose sightings in the early morning.

The route led to a 33-mile long old railroad bed that ran between Ashton and West Yellowstone. Idaho is a landlocked state. Perhaps the residents long for the shore because several miles of this path was like riding your bicycle at the beach, a slow spin through the sand. Spirits took a hit as flat riding became difficult.

57

The tires sank deeply into the black sandy volcanic soil. Steering was tough, more effort was needed in a slow pace. Sage and pine dominated the straight shot landscape. Beaver dams and ATVs were part of the scene. Motorcycles and moose shared the path. Lily pads, hundreds of them, grew in the waterways where the graceful white long necked trumpeter swans swam.

Though it's easy to use flowery prose to describe the scenery, inside things were boiling.

Relationships aren't easy. Compromise is constantly sought. Spending 24 hours a day, seven days a week with anyone is challenging whether there is love or not.

Being together all the time leads to statements like, "I love you, but I sure hate you right now."

Friendships are tested. Expectations collide. Everything is on display for each other to see. There's no place to hide when you're on the road together.

Humor can be a wonderful tool. It opens doors to smiles, temporarily eases a difficult situation, and creates ripples throughout the entire body when laughter erupts.

But it can also be used as sarcasm.

Hurry up and wait was my mantra. I had spent hundreds of miles looking over my shoulder, hoping Jan would show up already. It was hot. Patience ebbed. The climbs were hard. Though life on the road can be most rewarding, there is a lot of downtime. Sometimes riding can even get dull.

So, to use Jan's word, I started getting "mouthy."

Sarcasm started rearing its' ugly head. "It's about time you got here." "What took you so long?" Comments like that didn't help matters. When Jan would show up at a spot where I had been waiting for 10 minutes, I was all rested and ready to go. She wanted her rest time. I wasn't exactly on my best behavior.

So as the route turned tabletop flat and wheels crawled through the sand, Jan fell again.

She was near tears.

Instead of being supportive and consoling, biting commentary like "Can't you even stay on your bike" (or something like it) is not what you want to hear.

Jan does dish it back, but the situation can escalate into a most disgusting and unpleasant experience.

The flare-up was followed by silence. For nearly two hours, pushing our bikes, we trudged. Nothing was said. During that time, Jan was thinking about quitting, formulating a plan that would get her home after a visit to Yellowstone not that far ahead.

But those plans changed.

It started with a single word.

"Sorry."

Sorry for yelling. Sorry for cursing. Sorry for my sorry unsupportive self.

Humbling? Yes. But it's also effective.

What made Jan feel a lot better, not that I apologized profusely, was that I reminded her of my sorry white butt which all the world could see four days earlier on the Corinne-Bannack Road in Montana.

The road was once a wagon supply route that connected Bannack and its gold with the Union Pacific railroad in Corinne, Utah.

Ask Jan about it though and she'll say it was where I had "the shits."

Having consumed those Rocky Mountain Oysters and burritos back in Bannack, there was, as Winnie the Pooh might say, "a rumbly in my tumbly", the following morning. A glorious day it started to be. Jan was fueled, fired up, and ready to go. She was riding ahead of me, experiencing the joy of the day when she heard a scream.

"Jaaaaaaaaaaaaaaaaaaan," rang out over the marvelous barren scrub nothingness.

To add insult, Jan was at the top of a hill. Though she would head downhill, it also meant she would have to climb it again after she reached the source of the scream. With the adrenaline rush of an EMT worker racing to the scene, Jan hurried back down to find me standing in the scrub along a dirt road with my lycra bike shorts down around my ankles.

59

MARTY BASCH

"What's wrong?," she asked, concern still in her eyes before actually registering what she was seeing.

"Sweetheart, I've got the shits, and I've run out of toilet paper," I said.

"I'm finally ahead and you make me ride down the hill to give you toilet paper?," she said part in frustration, part in disbelief.

"Please," I said, throwing in a puppy dog look for some sympathy.

Finally realizing it wasn't a matter of life or death, but a matter of a few sheets, she took slow sadistic pleasure in the manufactured theatrics of trying to find the toilet paper she carried because being Jan, she knew exactly where everything was kept.

And being Marty, I stood with pants down in waiting under the grand western sky for the precious TP hoping no pickup truck would be going by anytime soon.

So fast forward to Idaho and the lesson learned that day. Be a man and say you're sorry, especially if the woman you love is going to have a story like "The Shits" to tell about you for the rest of your life.

After the apology, Idaho was a better place. The sand eventually faded away and we were riding again instead of walking.

It was also where Jan discovered the joys of wood gathering. Using trailers, it wasn't long before we discovered the rigs had many uses. One was as a table. On certain occasions we would unhook them from the bicycles,

IDAHO POTATO SOUP
Ingredients:
4 to 6 potatoes
1 onion, leek or scallion
1 pepper (red, green or yellow)
3 vegetable bullion cubes
salt, pepper, garlic powder
Directions:
Dice potatoes into 1/2 inch cubes. That way they'll cook as quickly as pasta. Dice onion and pepper. Sauté onion and pepper in pan. When onion is clear, add potatoes and bullion cubes. Cover with water and bring to boil. Simmer until potatoes fall apart. With fork, stir vigorously until potatoes are puree. Season to taste.

60

flip one over, put down a bandanna or two, and use it for a picnic table.

Jan had a hunkering for a campfire that night at the Warm River Campground in the Targhee National Forest. Neat and shaded, fly fishermen were out in the cool of the early evening, casting their poetic arc lines upon the waters.

I took my time getting there, stopping to take some photos of an old covered railroad bridge.

When I finally reached Jan down a hill, there was an addition to the load she was carrying: firewood.

Jan started picking up stray pieces of wood. Maybe they were pieces of wood left behind at campsites or had fallen out of a truck or just happened to be by the side of the road or trail. At first, I scoffed, calling her crazy. But later by the fire, I was calling her a genius. From that day on, if we knew were were within a few miles of our campsite for the night, we would stop for errant pieces of wood that would make a warming fire that night.

Though we learned a bit about ourselves in Idaho, there wasn't much gained in a sense of what Idaho is. The route shortchanged the red, white and blue license plate state. Whereas in Montana we met people from all walks of life, the only Idahoans we met were those behind a cash register. Aside from getting a taste of potatoes, there wasn't a chance to get a sense of who the people are, of how they live.

But if it were people that we wanted to see, we would soon have that chance, as the route left eastern Idaho for the Yellowstone-Teton swarm of Wyoming.

Chapter Eleven

The Tetons, Wyoming

Snow and summer meet in northwest Wyoming, home to the magnificent Tetons. It's also a place where dirt and pavement come together.

Ragtag road riders pedaling the paved cross-country TransAmerica Bicycle Trail and dusty mountain bikers can sit at the crossroads of dirt and hardtop at a couple of picnic tables outside a small general store and swap both stories and horseflies.

Bikers sometimes have no names in the brief exchanges among travelers. He was grubby, blonde, and from California. The guy was having a peanut butter and jelly sandwich outside that store when he saw us.

"You riding the Divide?," he asked.

"How can you tell?," Jan asked.

He motioned to the two mountain bikes and the one-wheeled trailers.

"Dirty," he said.

Dirty can come easy for intrepid cyclists. For about one month, we had been on the road, so we were dirty, and so was our gear. Montana was wet, wild and got us dirty. Idaho was a blip in the sand, and got us dirty too.

Now came Wyoming, the Cowboy State, where the terrain changes from high mountain meadows to dry fields of sage. No doubt we would get dirty here as well.

We sucked dust on the rough and rugged John D. Rockefeller

Jr. Parkway, a dirt road that saw its share of the summer swarm of tourists destined for the the Tetons and Yellowstone National Park. They came in RVs to watch the wildlife from the comfort of their motor homes. After the solitude of Idaho, the migration was a bit troubling as motorized vehicles kicked up enough dust on the dirt roads to give us our daily doses of vitamins and minerals.

ROCKY MOUNTAIN RAMEN

Ingredients:
1 pound hamburger
1 can of diced tomatoes and green chilies
1 tablespoon minced dried onions
2 garlic cloves
2 cups water
2 packages beef flavored ramen noodles

Directions:
In pan, place hamburger, dried onions and the two cloves of garlic that have been minced. Sauté until the meat is brown. Drain off excess fat. Add entire can of diced tomatoes with chilies and two cups water. Bring to a boil. Add broken packages of ramen noodles. Add beef seasoning as needed. Simmer until noodles are done.

Northwest Wyoming offered immense beauty though. Imagine spotting a bear cub from the seat of a bicycle by the side of a road. Stop at a picnic area and see a deer, no two, walk by. Look down into a meadow and see a moose look back. See reflections of the snow-capped peaks over 10,000 feet high in calm Jackson Lake.

Now imagine waiting in line to get into Yellowstone National Park. Then imagine waiting for a shower at the bustling Flagg Ranch. Then wait to get into another campground. Hurry up and wait.

That's Wyoming too.

We wanted no part of the summer tourist shuffle. See Wyoming today and drive to Colorado tomorrow. That seemed alien to a couple of bicycle travelers. A mindset develops when your means of propulsion is pedaling. You slow down. Your hearing becomes more acute, picking up the sounds of snapping branches, approaching vehicles, the wind. Taste buds become more appreciative, especially for sweets like ice cream.

Now our senses were being assaulted with the whirlwind of activity. We were tired. Our last night in Idaho hadn't been one filled with much sleep. Rowdy camp neighbors kept us awake and when they finally nodded off in a drunken stupor, Jan woke me up to investigate another noise.

There was a chewing sound outside the tent. Maybe the neighbors had the munchies, but that probably wasn't the case. Whatever it was, it was trying to gnaw its way into one of our packs. It didn't take much to scare it off. Imagine trying to have a midnight snack when a half-naked two-tone human shines a flashlight in your face. That's scary.

Six days of straight riding, averaging some 43 miles per day - a testament to Jan's increased strength - meant it was time for a break. We needed a day off. Hungry for a shower, we even passed up the opportunity for one of the eight free primitive campsites along the Rockefeller for the opportunity to plunk down $20 for a not-so-private campsite at the congested Flagg Ranch.

After setting up for a stay and taking a welcomed shower, it was a joy to then feast on an all-you-can-eat-damn-the-cholesterol fried chicken dinner while Jan opted for meat loaf in the comfort of a restaurant. Every meal wasn't a one pan Jan concoction.

Full and tired, we decided during the meal we would take the next day off to tend to the mundane matters of laundry and maybe do a little sightseeing. Sometimes the body just says stop. When it says feed me, give me some water, take a breather, run me until I drop, always listen to it.

Surrounded by the mountains, it was a pleasure to take both of our bodies' advice and doze off in the Wyoming night.

What made it even better was waking the next morning and not having to get into our morning routine of cook, roll up the bags, stuff the pads, take down the tent, etc. Instead, the campers next to us were preparing some French toast and offered us a chance to dig in which was accepted in a heartbeat - without couple consultation.

Fueled, we decided to check out the southern entrance of Yellowstone, about two miles away. We had to go by bike. That's kind of like stopping by the office on your day off just to pick up a file or something. It's not exactly the whole day off. How easy the bike maneuvered without all that weight of the trailer. When we learned it was about 22 miles inside the park before there was anything worth seeing, we decided to forget about it. The ranger told us the ride along the Tetons was better anyway. Old Faithful could blow off without us.

So we did laundry instead and those other mundane matters. Later on our camp neighbors Lane and Sherri happened to be cooking a chicken and potato dinner in a Dutch oven and invited us over. To see Jan not only have seconds, but thirds, is about as rare a sight as a Red Sox World Series victory celebration on the brick desert of Boston's City Hall Plaza. We slept well that night and opted for a short cycling day, a mere 18 miles, the next day. We wanted to spend more time in the tantalizing Tetons.

We cycled on pavement; highway filled with the swarm. Narrow shoulders on U.S. 287/191 meant we had to watch out for people in motorized vehicles who were looking for moose, deer or the splendid Tetons.

Motorhomes and cyclists can have uncomfortable relationships, especially with that extended passenger side mirror that can come along and bonk a biker's head. Everyone must drive or pedal defensively and all went well as the masses moved on. Tourists came in all modes of transportation. Heading for Colter Bay Village within the Grand Teton National Park, we saw all sorts of cyclists in the Tetons. Some waved. Some ignored us. A couple from Holland, biking America from end to end, crossed over from the other side of the road to chat with us. Not every cyclist is friendly, they were saying. They were proud of their homemade rain proof saddlebags and we exchanged information about what was ahead.

The ride was short, but magnificent and by ll a.m. we had already reached the campground.

And the line to get in.

It is not much fun to stand behind a group of motor vehicles with engines running as the exhaust spews out into your face. But that was what we did, taking in the novelty of being the lone cyclists in the line of traffic.

At the entrance, we found out there was a hiker/biker camping area for five bucks a head. We jumped at the opportunity, later learning that the campground was full by noon and no more motorized vehicles would be let in.

Plans called for a hike to see Mount Moran. Instead we succumbed to the movies at the visitor center (grizzlies, Indians, bison) and browsed through the Indian art museum, impressed by the detail in pieces that had survived a century.

Jan went shopping, picking up small souvenirs for loved ones back home. They were bike friendly gifts like earrings, necklaces, and refrigerator magnets. These were easy to carry until she mailed them home to herself. We had care packages waiting for us at various post offices along the route filled with different foods and spices (and precious new socks) Jan had packed before we left. She would then use the box to mail back anything she bought or gear we didn't think we needed anymore.

While she shopped, I headed into a restroom in search of an electric outlet to plug in the computer and do some work. There's nothing like going into the restroom to answer nature's call and seeing a guy sitting on the floor, doing the keyboard dance.

When I returned to the campsite, Jan was there. She had a six-pack surprise and we enjoyed being the lone campers in the biker/hiker area that night, as the swarm snored around us.

Chapter Twelve

The Tetons to Lander, Wyoming

Route 287 leads cyclists away from the Tetons and the masses. Soon the pavement was left for the gentle, quiet, and rolling Buffalo Valley Road outside of Moran Junction. Rolling roads often lead to hills and we climbed up into the Bridger-Teton National Forest.

Seven times the Divide is crossed in the Cowboy State. Each one can kick like the bronc on the state license plates. Togwotee Pass, at 9,658 feet in the Shoshone National Forest, is the highest on the route. Though it has a kick, it is a relatively easy ride on pavement. But it was a return to grizzly country and the bear spray was placed on ready.

Complacence was a memory on the grueling dirt Union Pass which winds and slithers with steep grades up to alpine meadows at 9,210 feet, making it feel like you are riding on top of the world. There we met a woman from California with two kids, who had stopped at the same place for a picture. That theory of Six Degrees of Separation, where everyone is linked by six people, works well on a bike trip. She had, a week before, met Jim and Dale from New Hampshire, the cyclists we had met in Seeley Lake, Montana on Independence Day.

What goes up, does go down - eventually. Each pass has its

own personality. Some provide the downhill award immediately, while others like to make you push up one more ridge before doling out the prize.

Though Montana claims the big sky as its own, it's just as big in Wyoming. Afternoon thunderstorms are one way to set one's watch in the West and around 3 p.m. or so, they would come. Not just rain, but hail too.

In cycling through Wyoming, brilliant Indian paintbrush, cattle guards and even stop signs outnumber the towns through which you pass. On paper, it's about 230 miles between Colter Bay Village and Atlantic City. There isn't much. But it's excellent preparation for the desert stretch across the Great Divide Basin between Atlantic City and Rawlins where you go from not much to nothing.

But first, there's Cora in Sublette County, south of the Wind River mountains. If you were lucky enough to meet postal worker LuAnne Freeman you might get a short tour of the post office (built in 1898), adjacent saloon (it's closed) and house (quite quaint). The Place, a small restaurant and bar on Route 352 outside the Bridger-Teton National Forest, served up Denver omelets and milk shakes. The bar is also custom West - horns, heads and hides on the wall.

In Pinedale, cyclists just seem to be pulled to the cinnamon rolls at Sue's Bread Box. Riders must stock up on groceries and water whenever they can.

Are there bike shops? Not exactly. Try the back of a hardware store in Pinedale after a 61 mile day. My rear wheel was getting a bit wobbly and not being skilled much in bike repair beyond fixing a flat tire and maybe using the pump to hit something in order to fix it or wrapping something in duct tape, I have learned it is best to seek help if available. We learned of a hardware store with a bike shop in the back. That's where we met Dale Hall in the first bike shop we had seen since Butte, Montana, about 500 miles away.

Bespectacled and mustached, Hill replaced two spokes, readjusted my derailleur, and trued the wheel.

He also gave us an idea of what lay ahead on the Divide.

Like many people we met, Hill offered an alternative to what was on the map. But Jan and I agreed to stick to the route.

The man knew what he was talking about.

From Pinedale to Boulder, riders get to play an 18 mile game of follow the fence line. Most of the roads on the Great Divide route have some sort of sign. That wasn't the case here. This is a place where roads have no names. Ruts, two-track, bedrock, velvety sand, five-way signless junctions and sticky mud gumbo all intertwine as cyclists must make their way between the two communities. There is a raw beauty cycling through the saddles of mountains but it is also maddening when it's possible to look down and see the smooth, pavement of highway 191 on the other side of the New Fork River. The Divide ride is no straight line. First zig, then zag. Then do it again.

After four hours in the sage-laden mesas, there finally was pavement, sweet brilliant pavement that meant civilization. Civilization, at this point, meant a soda machine.

Here, the directions on the map told us to go one way, but it was wrong, leading us two miles to nowhere until we collected our wits, retraced our tracks and got back on the route.

Apparently we weren't the only ones confused about where to go because a note on a post caught our eyes. It was for Alex.

We knew him.

Alex, it said, with an arrow. Three miles, it said. Alex was the driver of the white van. That meant Team DeSisto was ahead, the girls from the Stockbridge, Massachusetts high school we had met in Bannack, Montana.

As we neared the Little Sandy Creek campground and its' shady groves of pine and aspen, the girls were there, cheering us on.

That night we re-counted our adventures over a spaghetti dinner and Jan exchanged knitting tales with one of the girls, Jackie, who lived south of us in New Hampshire.

It was a chance to chat with Tiffany Harris, a teacher and the group leader.

MARTY BASCH

"It is much, much more challenging to ride on dirt and to negotiate downhills and gravel where there are half buried rocks, fallen timber and that kind of thing," she said. "Even the cattle guards at first spooked us a little bit."

The campground, is near the 1,000 mile mark on the ride and she broke the trip down into the first 500 and second 500 miles. The first was very intense with some of the girls having a rough time. She had to remind them that they had chosen to go on the trip.

Like many riders, the early part of a trip was drudgery because they weren't in shape. It was tough. Plus there was rain, lots of northern Montana rain.

There was one of the girls who fell and broke her arm. She was traveling in the van.

"Then when we got into the southern part of the state, the weather changed and that really coincided with a major change in attitude and skill level," she said. "Since then, the group has been a lot more cohesive and it has just been a lot more fun."

Coyotes, beavers, deer, fox and moose were all part of the scenery, not all commonplace for the Eastern-based riders.

"It's been beautiful," she said. Then she recalled the day they rode into Union Pass.

"Most of us are from cities on the East Coast," she said. "I had never been able to see so far. I couldn't believe it when we rode into the fields of sage and then we just saw people riding carefree on these horses. It was really like something I had only seen on television."

That night was the last time we would see the girls, so we took our photos, shared our memories, and got some shuteye.

I needed rest. Though I didn't know it yet, I was about to descend into bicycle hell.

The day into hell began as the Wind River Range started to disappear. A tantalizingly long grunt up South Pass followed and we rode into South Pass City, a ghost town opened to tourists. The climbs into Atlantic City were also a chore and it was there, hell welcomed me.

70

In Atlantic City, there is no boardwalk, no salt water taffy and no Donald Trump, though there is a bartender named Don at one of the two restaurants in the community of 25 year-round residents.

There was also the scream.

I was the cause of that scream. With one stroke of the pedal, my world became hell. There was a loud metallic shriek. Then my bike stopped. I followed with a string of profanities.

The rear derailleur had sliced into five spokes rendering me both spokeless and clueless as to what to do. Just two days before my bike had been repaired. Now Jan tried to calm me down as I unleashed a verbal hurricane.

Shutting my eyes, counting to three and then opening

The turns are many along the Great Divide.

them did not fix the problem. Nor did hurling a pump at the bike. Duct tape wouldn't work.

I was royally, totally screwed.

Though it would have been nice to head into a bar and forget all about it, that wasn't the bright thing to do.

Then came the pickup truck.

It passed by once.

We hardly noticed.

But a few minutes later, it came by again.

"Need a ride?," asked the driver.

Indeed we did, we told the man we would later call the Atlantic City Angel. Fittingly, he drove a white pickup truck. His name was Chuck. Chuck happened to own some property in Atlantic City and was on his way home to Riverton, wherever that was. We said we would like to go to Lander, about 35 miles away. We were going there for a couple of reasons. The primary reason was so that Jan could have a mother and daughter reunion and the second was because there was a bike shop that would, hopefully, have a tech who would take me out of derailleur hell.

That was no problem for Chuck. First we headed into the Sagebrush Saloon and Cafe for a much appreciated thirst quencher or two and then let the Atlantic City Angel drive the way over the stunningly beautiful red hills on Route 28 north to Lander, which happened to be on the way to Riverton.

There in Lander, the angel led us to a motel, said good-bye and like many other strangers who had intervened on our behalf, headed off into the sunset.

He left us exactly where we wanted, and needed, to be.

Chapter Thirteen

Lander, Wyoming to the Colorado border

The loneliest stretch of Wyoming along the Great Divide Mountain Bike Route is the wasteland between the outpost of Atlantic City and the wind-ravaged town of Rawlins.

Before setting out into the abyss where water is a concern for 140 or so miles, cyclists fill up at either the Sagebrush or the Mercantile, top off the water bottles and purchase limited, last minute groceries.

Then, they take the plunge across the wide open Great Divide Basin where the Continental Divide splits and forms a circle where water doesn't drain. It just sits and evaporates.

There are no stores across the Basin, and there is very little water.

But there is water in Lander, where the Atlantic City Angel had dropped us. The town of 7,000 had stores, too, and was home to the National Outdoor Leadership School or NOLS, a top wilderness training facility.

The Maverick Motel was now the center of our universe. From its Main Street location, Jan waited on the last Friday in July for her 15 year-old daughter Jena and fifty-something friend Bobbie Box to make the long, exhausting trip from North Conway, New Hampshire. First it was a flight to Denver and then the hand-

73

MARTY BASCH

numbing 350 mile drive or so across the Western nothingness to
Lander just to spend the weekend.

From the motel, I walked my hobbled bike down Main Street
- and also ran some errands like dropping off film, buying water
filters, etc. - to Freewheel Ski and Cycle where I could complain
about my troubles to sympathetic souls.

In less than an hour, a new chain guard was installed, six
spokes replaced (three additional ones were given to me for
emergencies), the wheel trued and derailleur re-adjusted.

To be on the safe side - it's easy for a bike shop to wave good-
bye to a customer traveling by bike because chances are they won't
see each other again - I took the bike for a spin. The gears didn't
shift quite right and the bike tech then made some adjustments.

I was now, thanks in part to the Atlantic City Angel, out of
bicycle hell.

Every cyclist will pick the brain of bike shop employees. Jan
and I had serious concerns about crossing the Basin. Not only
now, but before the trip started. Jan doesn't do heat well. I lived
in the Middle East and when I heard the word "desert" it conjured
up images of camels, the occasional palm tree oasis, savage wind
storms, and sand that infiltrates everything. Not that the Great
Divide Basin would be the Sahara, but the mind can devise enough
pre-ride tricks to make you crazy.

So the guy at the bike shop, hearing my pre-crossing jitters -
because I was worried about Jan of course - suggested I give Ray
Hanson a call.

Ray's the man.

That's because he is the man who mapped out the section of the
Divide we were about to ride.

An avid cyclist and longtime Adventure Cycling Association
member, Hanson worked as an outdoor recreation planner with
the Bureau of Land Management in Lander. He had an idea for the
route through the Great Divide Basin and when he learned about
the Great Divide, he contacted ACA and Mike McCoy. In 1996,
he and McCoy drove the route. The next year, Hanson, Rawlins'
dentist Jeff Sweet and fellow BLM employee Karla Swanson

pedaled their way across the high desert.

So, I called Hanson.

Not only did he return the call, but he showed up at our hotel to drive us to his office where we sat going over maps while an afternoon thunder boomer outside caused the lights inside to flicker.

We chatted about the road ahead and Hanson's involvement in the route.

"(We) primarily chose this route because of public access roads," said Hanson. "That was one of the primary conditions. Adventure Cycling was going to utilize public access roads so there was no need to ask permission from private landowners. There was no need to acquire easements and as a BLM outdoor recreation planner I took it upon myself to assist Mac (Mike McCoy) in his quest to make the route and basically used my knowledge of the area."

It was nice to hear Hanson knew what he was talking about because he had ridden the route.

"I decided before I recommended this to anybody to ride, we better ride it," he said. "So I recruited some friends and the three of us did a two day ride from the South Pass/Atlantic City area to Rawlins and figured it was doable if we could do it."

Hanson's insight was great relief to us. As he drove us back to the motel, we made plans to hook up with him and his wife Mary Saturday night for dinner.

Back at the room, Jan and I were discussing the next leg of the trip when she heard familiar voices in the motel courtyard. In an instant she transformed from biker babe to mobile mom, bolting out the door and rushing down the stairs to greet, hug, and eventually crush both Bobbie and Jena as they made their way to the room from the rental car.

Jan needed to recharge her motherly batteries. The weekend was a whirlwind of catching up and going places. It was a chance to go through about five weeks of mail (mostly junk), wear clothes for a weekend that had been brought from home (an absolute trail pleasure), and marvel at how fast the world could go by at

MARTY BASCH

60 miles per hour as we played tourists on the Wind River Indian
Reservation, Sinks Canyon, and South Pass City. It was also a joy
to see yet another Easterner hesitate before crossing that first cattle
guard, even if it were in a car. We too were uncertain about riding
over our first one. That's okay. We love to watch Westerners eat
their first lobster.

With a constant score of Estrogen 3, Testosterone 1, there was
a lot of shopping involved too. We ate out (with the Hansons too
on Saturday night, where it was decided they would drive our bikes
and gear out to Atlantic City on Sunday, as the rental car couldn't
fit everyone and everything), had indoor plumbing, and loved not
setting up the tent.

Sunday appeared and the less-than-48 hour visit came and went
with tears, hugs, and promises as yet another car moseyed off into
the sunset as both a happy and sorrow-to-see-them-go Jan and I
walked our way up and out of Atlantic City on an afternoon start
and into the void.

RAWLINS RICE & ROOSTER

Ingredients:
3/4 pound boneless chicken
1 small white onion
1/4 pound of white mushrooms
2 tablespoons of lemon pepper seasoning
2 cups instant rice
2 cups water

Directions:
Cut chicken in thin strips and toss with
lemon pepper seasoning. Dice onion in 1/2
inch pieces and slice mushrooms. Heat pan
and add chicken. Stir occasionally. Add
onions and mushrooms. Sauté until onions
are almost transparent. Add water, bring
to boil. Add rice. Stir, cover tightly. Shut
off heat. Wait five minutes. Savor the
flavor!

We had three
gallons of water with
us. At eight pounds
per gallon that's 24
additional pounds.
Hanson had also told
us where to look
for water along the
way. We decided on
a three day Basin
crossing of 12, 72
and 55 miles.

The Oregon and
California Trails
once ran in the Basin.
Pioneers in stage
coaches and wagon
trains once traveled
over the sage to reach the West. Keen eyes can see the swales of

the tracks. Most just romanticize about what once was.

En route to the Sweetwater River (a guaranteed water source), we met a rancher who told us how he once helped a cyclist overcome muscle cramps. Before we knew it, we were at the river and bumped into 11 cyclists from a North Carolina summer camp and two from Colorado, Roger and Kathy Cox, whom we would bump into again.

The next day was an early start, before 7 a.m.

We would not reach a place to bed down for the night until 13 hours later.

The desert is supposed to be a hot, sandy place. At least that was the vision. This desert was cloudy, cold and rainy. Fleece, gloves and rain slickers were worn instead of a t-shirt, baseball cap and sunscreen.

The desert was not flat, but rather hilly. The wind was brutal, forcing us to five miles per hour. The road wasn't silky, but rough and washboarded. The clouds darkened over the vastness and we watched the rains come our way, set up above us, and drench us below.

Nonetheless water was on our minds as we saw more pronghorns, wild horses, and grouse than people. It is said there are more pronghorns than people in Wyoming. This is true in the Basin. The animals are graceful, running in uniform formation with white-tails bouncing.

To see a wild horse is amazing too. Their unkempt tails nearly reach the ground and their manes are long and unruly. The stallions mark their territory by depositing foot-high piles of manure.

The Divide will change your mind about water. Outdoor taps and campground hand pumps are a luxury. Along the Divide, it is routine to filter water from creeks or plop in purification tablets or boil it. Sometimes you do all three.

But then, creeks become luxuries too. Because on the Divide, riders will have to draw water from containers, tubs, and tanks meant for animals like cattle and horses.

We came across our first one maybe ten miles into the day, alerted to it by Ray Hanson. It was a bathtub with a red hose in it.

Over time, we would come to appreciate seeing water tanks and drinking from the same trough as a mooing side of beef that one day would make it to the dinner table.

Not only did we have to contend with the foul weather and drawing water from stock tanks, we crashed too.

Descending a hill, Jan caught a rut and launched herself over her handlebars onto the dirt road. I was following too closely, slammed on the brakes to avoid her, and ended up over my handlebars as well.

I scraped my left knee while Jan was a bit more banged up, bloodying both knees, and scraping a thigh. We administered first aid to ourselves, our scrapes not as bad as they could have been because we were wearing our shells which protected our skin from the rough road.

We were okay, but Jan had a total body ache and her knees felt as if they were in a plaster cast. The winds did not abate and tears, fueled by the fall and the difficulty of the day, ran down her cheeks.

But a smile did return. Though a 72 mile day in the desert isn't exactly a day at the beach, there was joy found in a desert rainbow or the grouse hiding in the scrub. Fortune sometimes even came our way with the wind finally at our backs. We rode down a hill to the shores of the A&M Reservoir and set up camp as darkness fell.

Sleep came quickly until Jan woke me up. She heard noise.

She didn't believe me when I suggested it was the wind. She twice checked the alcove area outside the tent for intruders. She found none.

That is until daylight. Detective Duprey examined the evidence at the crime scene. Some nocturnal creature had the munchies again and chewed some of our garbage.

We were hurting puppies that morning. The wind did not abate. Procrastination with tea, coffee and cream of wheat was the morning's activity. Still we were back on the bikes just after eight. The riding was joyous the first fifteen miles, pronghorns greeting us. When we turned onto pavement, the wind slapped us around again.

Then the trucks took their turn about 15 miles out of the city of Rawlins, trying to knock us off our bikes as they generated even more wind gusts. Rawlins, with a population of about 8,500, was incorporated in 1886 and is the county seat in Carbon County.

We were back in the land of conveniences. We found a campground, showered, did laundry, caught up on columns, and were able to walk across the street to a restaurant for dinner after completing our ride across the desert.

In a neighborhood with the grunt of trucks from Interstate 80, a train station, and a main street converging around us, we didn't get much sleep again though no rodent tried to get into our food supply that night.

After the Basin's wrath, we were exhausted and didn't know it. We started drinking more water more quickly as we pedaled closer to the Colorado border and a welcome return to the trees.

Cycling south of Rawlins we stumbled across the kindness of strangers. In the course of about three miles up the final Divide crossing in the state - Middlewood Hill - people behind the steering wheel stopped to offer assistance as we pushed our bikes up the never-ending hill. One was a Game and Fish biologist who topped off our water bottles. The second was a couple of locals who offered us a ride. We declined. The third was a woman who offered us a place to stay for the night. We thanked her but wanted to continue.

Walking side by side is also a good time for some heart-to-heart talks between couples. Exhaustion and frustration can bring out tempers, but also some intimate thoughts and feelings. We were nearly to the halfway point of the trip and we had learned a few things.

We were still talking to each other. This was good. The key to being a happy cycling couple can be summed up with the three c's - communication, compromise and chocolate.

Communication is a must. If you don't talk, you become stagnant. If she insists on asking strangers for directions, let her. Women do that sort of thing. It's okay.

And another thing. If you are standing together and she turns around for a minute and then turns back around and you're not there, she'll get upset. Should you decide to, say, go into a store or go for a walk, tell her first. Women need that sort of thing.

Again, this is called communication.

Compromise is an important tenet of the outdoor relationship game. Let's say she wants to have a fire at night and you balk at the idea of shelling out three bucks for an armload of wood. The next day she still wants a fire at night, but this time she doesn't ask. Instead, about five miles from the campsite, she starts stopping to pick up pieces of firewood from the roadside. Upon arrival at the campsite, there is wood to be burned.

Of course, let's say you laugh when she does this wood scavenger thing. You may say something like it's ridiculous and she just flashes you a murderous look.

That night you enjoy the tranquility of the fire.

The next day you become a wood scavenger too. You feel like a macho backwoodsman because western wood is bone dry and lights with one match.

This is called compromise.

Cleanliness is something we compromised on. During my solo cycling trips, laundry twice a month seemed fine with me. Then again, I was always riding by myself. Jan has this thing about staying clean. If there's a creek, she had to wash her clothes. We averaged two loads a week in laundrymats. She also despises those small boxes you buy at the spin and suds. We actually bought a box of detergent and divided it into little plastic bags for each load. This weighed maybe three pounds. But we saved a few bucks.

Again, this is called compromise.

When compromise and communication fail, there is chocolate. Let's suppose during certain discussions, communication breaks down. There can be silence or there can be harsh words. Silence is okay. You can't get into a lot of trouble. But say the wrong thing and there's no place to hide. That is, unless there is chocolate at the next store. If there is, buy her lots. She'll eat it because she's burning more calories than ever before.

She might even save some for you to shove in your mouth the

next time you say something on the stupid side.

It's a good idea to carry lots of chocolate if you are cycling with a woman you love.

No chocolate was needed that night as we slept in the forest at a primitive campground after a tough 35 mile day. It was our last night in Wyoming. We were dry camping too. Gone was carrying that extra three gallons of water, a burdening 24 pounds. We were back to topping off at every tap and water source we found.

We found we could also beg for water.

Parked within sight of our tent was a truck. On it, I left a note for its owners to wake us if they had any water. Hardly able to keep our eyes open as darkness fell, around 9 p.m. we were awakened by the lights of a truck and a rumble of the engine. The owner had returned, and before even reading the note, woke us up with the roar of the engine. There was water and we had a bit of a crusty eyed conversation, but thanked the two and tried to sleep again.

Our final day in the Cowboy State, August 7, we left the high desert for the green splendor of the Medicine Bow National Forest. We cycled through the glory of "aspen alley" and then delighted in the 13 mile descent on Highway 70 through the Sierra Madre Range.

When we reached the Colorado border we passed the midway point of the trip. To paraphrase the poet Robert Frost, we still had many more miles to go.

Chapter Fourteen

Colorado border to Steamboat Springs

Somewhere along the Wyoming-Colorado border we passed the milestone. It's a little tough to pinpoint exactly which state we were in because the snaking dirt road danced between the two states. The sage of Wyoming was on the left and the green of Colorado on the right.

Nonetheless, after nearly 1,230 miles we reached the midpoint of the Route and were halfway home.

In Colorado, we rode by slender aspens and tall, wavy pines. It was hard to imagine with a plush, green ski area in the distance that just a few days ago we were were battling the cold and wind of Wyoming's high country desert.

The road to Steamboat went through the Routt National Forest and by the tiny town of Columbine in the shadows of Hahns Peak. Columbine had a year-round population of about four families and a general store with a wood stove where the owners were kind enough to load us up from their private stock of tangerines and cherries when we wanted some fresh produce instead of canned nourishment. This was not the same Columbine where in April 1999 two high school students massacred fellow students, teachers and administrators. That was in Littleton, a Denver suburb, and when we were riding the Divide, the Columbine shootings hadn't happened yet.

Not everyone riding the Divide will pass through Columbine on the way to Steamboat, home of Billy Kidd, the Vermont-native, cowboy hat wearing, double medal winning, Olympic skier. There are times the Divide Route offers riders a choice. There is the main route and several alternate routes on occasion. The main Divide Route followed Route 70 in Wyoming and headed into Slater on the Wyoming-Colorado border. We didn't do that. All it took was the suggestion of a couple of locals we met. The way through Columbine was gorgeous, they said. You shouldn't miss it, they said. On the map, it said the alternate route was four miles shorter, had slightly more traffic, and was a potentially dusty road. That way was also beautiful, according to the map. But it was one word that convinced Jan and me to take it: easier.

We took the excellent advice from the locals. So much for not taking an alternate route during the trip.

We rejoined the main route after cycling the shores of Steamboat Lake and returned to pavement in Clark where we met yet another local who had an impact on our trip.

We'll call him Harry. That's not his real name of course, and there he was at the Clark Store as we were, and he was on his bicycle - a recumbent. Jan had never seen one before. It's one of those rigs where you sit down in a real seat in a reclining position and pedal two wheels.

Local cyclists are welcome resources and Harry, who lived down the road in Steamboat, suggested we try a campground in town, though it being a Saturday in August, there was a chance it would be booked. But he did promise he would stop by later that night and we could join him and his wife, we'll call Sally, for dinner.

Into the glitz of Steamboat Springs we rode. There was running water from faucets, toilets with plumbing, supermarkets, and bike shops. Steamboat was swarming with tourists. It was a chance to get off the bikes for a day or so and utilize the free shuttle bus to get around town. With a packed but not filled campground there was no shortage of adjacent campers willing to drive us around town for errands too.

Promptly at 7 p.m. Harry and Sally tracked us down amidst the cacophony of campers. We went, via motor vehicle, in search of a restaurant where we exchanged stories of adventure and the love of the bicycle. Harry was a writer and photographer. He and Sally were talking about an upcoming trip to Antarctica. Cooking was a passion too, and it was decided the next day Harry would pick us up in the afternoon, show us around the area, and dinner would be at their house. It was a done deal.

First we had to deal with the mundane activities that come with a rest day. Things needed to get done, like making a beeline for the campground's Sunday three dollar all-you-can-eat pancake breakfast, complete with coffee, small apple juice and two sausages. We also had to call our mothers. No matter how old you are, if you go on a bike trip, call your mother. She'll still worry, but at least she'll feel better.

Columns and newsletters needed to be written and e-mailed. Shopping had to be done. The bikes had to be brought in for the mid-ride tune-up, thankfully fitting in the back of a fellow camper's pickup truck for the drive to the Sore Saddle Cyclery at the corner of 12th and Yampa, by the Yampa River.

The shop is in a dome, an old wood chip incinerator the owner bought from the city for a buck and moved to its downtown location, not far from Howelsen Hill, a training ground for ski jumpers.

There we dropped off the bikes and then moseyed around town for a while. Eventually we returned to the bike shop where we met a couple of locals outside. Talk turned to our trip and we told them about the couple we had met and gone to dinner with.

"Did they pay for it?," one of them asked.

Odd question, I thought. We explained we split the meal, though Harry and Sally picked up the tab for wine.

It was then we learned that Harry and Sally were Powerball winners and had moved to Steamboat from the midwest after their good fortune.

Just how does someone bring up the topic of lottery winners

at dinner? Harry showed up at the campsite later that afternoon.

Before heading to his home, we took a drive to do a short walk to Fish Creek Falls on the southern part of town. The raging water plunges over 280 feet down between a rock gateway surrounded by the thickness of the evergreen forest. A popular stop on the tourist trail, it was a short quarter mile to the falls. We weren't alone of course. The U.S. Forest Service estimates there are some 100,000 visitors to the falls annually. Sure, but how many of them can say they were driven there by a Powerball winner?

From the falls it was up to Harry and

STEAMBOAT STEW

Ingredients:
1 pound stew meat
1 medium onion
1 small turnip
2 large potatoes
2 carrots
2 stalks celery
1 handful fresh green beans
1 package instant brown gravy
water
1/2 tablespoon oil
1/2 cup red wine (optional)
1 tablespoon Worcestershire sauce

Directions:
Dice meat into one inch cubes. Clean and cut all vegetables into 1/2 to one inch pieces. Set aside. Heat large pot and add the oil to sear the meat. Deglaze pan with the red wine or water. Add potatoes, carrots, turnip and celery. Cover with water and let simmer about 15 minutes. When vegetables are almost done, add the onion and green beans. If necessary, add more liquid to cover ingredients. Simmer until vegetables are done and meat is tender. Add package of instant gravy to thicken. This is a hearty pot of stew and can be enjoyed with the remaining red wine.

Sally's, where Sally was waiting. The hillside home overlooked the verdant green slopes of Steamboat where no doubt in winter the plumes of rooster tails from skiers hooting it up on powder days can be seen. But on this evening, the only birds were those attracted to the hummingbird feeders. Appetizers, beer, wine, hamburger soup and bread were all part of a wonderful evening of stories.

The conversation never did get around to Lady Luck, so as far as we know, and still want to think now, they were just a friendly couple who decided to share their hospitality with a couple of strangers along the Divide.

Though Harry's words - something like, we are ordinary people with extraordinary circumstances - sure made sense.

Not only did we meet strangers along the Divide, we also saw familiar faces. Though better in person, this one peered out to me from the pages of *Steamboat Today* on the morning after we had dinner with Harry and Sally. This was the summer Bill Clinton was rewording the definition of sex and there was yet another story on Independent Counsel Kenneth Starr's quest to impeach the president after his tryst with Monica Lewinsky. But it wasn't the wire story that caught my attention on the Monday morning we were leaving Steamboat.

It was the photo on page 23, next to the massage ad.

There was Carl Swenson signing autographs. Those who consider sports to be done with balls and blades may be unfamiliar with Swenson. He is a two-sport athlete: mountain biking and cross-country skiing. A cross-country skiing Olympian, he grew up in North Conway, N.H. where his parents Steve and Sally - no relation to Harry and Sally - live. Steve and Sally have helped me numerous times by recommending bike and ski trails for books I've written. I've interviewed Carl and met him a few times.

And it seems of late than when I go on a bike trip, there's the Swenson connection.

In 1996, it was in Norway, near the Russian border. I happened upon an athlete training on roller skis. He stopped for a rest and we chatted. Turns out he was on the Norwegian National Ski Team and he knew Carl from competition.

So here it was two years later and there was that Swenson connection again. Carl had been in Steamboat that weekend competing in the Mercury Tour mountain bike race. He won Sunday's gondola criterium stage.

And we had yet another small world tale to tell.

Chapter Fifteen

Steamboat Springs to Summit County, Colorado

The nearly 130 miles from Steamboat Springs into Summit County ran through small towns like Radium and Kremmling and by mountains like the Gore Range. It also was a ragtag ride of emotions as we went from flat, easy pedaling to sucking wind through Lynx Pass at 8,937 feet. Luckily those passes came with the rewards of scintillating downhills on the other side.

Though August, elevation meant cold. That could mean good sleeping weather, but it also means fleece and cuddling a little closer in the tent.

At a campground in Lynx Pass, about 40 miles from Steamboat, we ran into a cycling Colorado couple named Roger and Kathy. They looked familiar. Turns out we had all met back in Wyoming in the Great Divide Basin also while camping.

We would, over the duration of the rest of the trip, travel together from time to time, doing what most long-distance cyclists love to do: save money on overnights.

We wouldn't ride together all the time. Sometimes it was just for a couple of hours. Sometimes we would catch up for lunch.

Other times we would meet up at a campsite at the end of the day, like in Kremmling where we camped out behind the town police station.

After the bustle of Steamboat, plain old Kremmling was the right spot to call it a night after the trials and tribulations of a myriad of surfaces, hills and splendid canyon vistas.

Not that anyone would have known it had I not opened my mouth, but this wasn't the first time I had been in this town of some 1200 or so. In 1992, I had gone on a nearly five month solo bicycle tour of the American Southwest and parts of Mexico. On Memorial Day weekend of that year, I found myself along with a fellow cyclist named John from California, in Kremmling on a holiday Saturday.

That morning a thin layer of frost sat atop the tent and handlebar bag, but quickly melted as the sun rose. We were cycling our third mountain pass in as many days, Gore Pass at 9,527 feet on paved State Highway 40, and descended the snakelike road with reverse hairpin turns into a valley with the mighty white peaks of the Rocky Mountain National Park in the distance.

We picked up U.S Route 40, the TransAmerica Bicycle Trail, and rode into Kremmling where we sought out the tourist information center. There we found out about the various camping opportunities and were told we could pitch a tent for free behind the police station or pay for a site at an RV park.

It being a holiday and we being in a small town, we wondered if there might be any activities that day like a parade, a barbecue, or a softball game between the fire department and police department. We asked the woman in the center if there were such a thing.

She told us no.

Desperate for some form of entertainment, she was asked again if anything was going on in town.

She paused and thought for a moment.

"Well, there is a funeral and I bet you would be welcome," she said.

Having not brought our Sunday best, we opted to pass on the

funeral but we did go next door to an old one-room cabin, the site of the former town jail. Inside, the walls were covered with black and white photographs of days gone by, including a shot of the 1925 Kremmling high school basketball team. Folks looked damn mean and ugly back then. They never smiled much.

Also looking at history's melancholy faces was a couple who appeared to be in their 60s.

"I get tired just looking at those bikes," the woman said about our rigs leaning outside. We started speaking with them, telling them about bicycling, and also asked them if there were anything in the town for us to do. Maybe they knew about some chicken barbecue fundraiser for the local Little League or something.

They didn't.

They left, and soon enough, so did we.

As we were about to mount the bikes, the man with a nicely rounded stomach, handed John a twenty dollar bill.

"Here, have dinner on us tonight," he said.

We were too stunned to say anything but thank you and John, to use his favorite expression, was stoked. The couple then drove off.

Armed with newfound wealth, these were 1992 dollars remember, we opted for the RV park on the eastern edge of town and the showers it contained, as it had been a week since the last one.

Clean again, it was time for a huge chicken dinner at the Wagon Restaurant, for the best chicken fried steak I had ever had in Kremmling.

For old-time sake, we were back in the Wagon - Jan, Roger, Kathy and myself - a short spin from the back of the jail where we were camping that night. There they listened to my tale of John, the funeral invitation and the twenty dollar bill.

Though the chicken fried steak that night was good and the happy hour a welcome way to begin the evening's festivities, it will never be as good as the one that lives in my memory on that Saturday in 1992.

The next morning, Jan and I were ready to hit the road. First,

we had to make a call from a pay phone. It was time to call Jay
O'Neal in Concord, N.H. at New Hampshire Public Radio.

As Jay sat in a warm studio thousands of miles away, Jan and I
sipped on hot coffees in the chill of a Colorado morning by a street
side pay phone.

Whether it was Jay in Concord or George Cleveland (grandson
of President Grover Cleveland) at WMWV radio in North Conway
or Amy Quigley (now Mahoney) at Resort Sports Network also
in the Mount Washington Valley, it was always a pleasure to call
in and hear a friendly voice. Jan didn't feel that way initially as
the idea of being on radio or television rattled her a bit. But as the
miles wore on, she became more relaxed about being on the air.

This day with Jay I chatted about the well-maintained dirt
roads of Colorado, the elevation changes and the number of
cyclists we were seeing (more in one day than the entire time spent
in Montana).

Then it was Jan's turn on the phone. The conversation turned to
spills along the way and she confessed about the crash in the Great
Divide Basin.

"...I hit a rut and lost control," she said. "And I guess I went
under, over, did a nice little slide. Both knees look like I've been in
a roller derby."

Jay then laughed.

"Then Marty crashed right behind me.... He's okay and my
bruises have healed so I'm alive, I'm talking to you and I'm still
pedaling so...."

"That's good," Jay said. "How's the chow wagon?"

"The chow wagon is fine," she said. "We're eating lots of
pasta, lots of rice....We've been doing a lot of pasta because that
gives you a lot of carbohydrates and energy. A couple of days ago,
we were in Steamboat and I did a Steamboat stew. I had access to
a large supermarket, picked up vegetables, even a bottle of wine.
When I browned my meat I deglazed it with some burgundy and
then stirred in the vegetables because we had more time. So we
had this nice pot of stew with a little wine on the side."

"I do smell a cookbook coming out of this Jan," said Jay.

"I hope so. I do hope so," she said. "I'm collecting all my daily recipes, just jotting them down...."

After hanging up with Jay, we had food on the brain. Going into a grocery store with Jan is never quick. She looks at items down the aisles like visitors to an art museum might study the paintings and sculptures in its spaces. Whenever we travel to ethnic neighborhoods, whether it be New York's Chinatown or Boston's North End, there is always a stop in a grocery store or bakery. Sometimes we just browse.

That morning Jan went into the grocery store - as part of being a couple, we found sometimes it is best that Jan go into the store by herself while I loiter outside - to pick up goodies for the haul up the pass and down into Summit County.

Fresh fruit and vegetables are always welcome. But Jan did it again. Remember, this is a woman who made us split up a large box of laundry soap to carry, the person who introduced me to firewood scavenging, and who managed to carry an always refreshing wet wash cloth to wipe the trail dust from our faces' nooks and crannies each night.

That morning, Jan taught me about defrosting.

Among the items she carried out in the sack to be thrown in with our gear was a fat and frozen package of Jimmy Dean sausage.

Roger and Kathy, who were also getting supplies, couldn't believe what they were seeing either. Okay, if we're camping in town and the store has some meat, let's buy it and fry it right away. But carry a package of pork in your pack all day so that it can melt and be cooked campside later that night?

That is insanity!

And that is why Jan spent the day biking with Mr. Jimmy Dean. Jimmy got a ride to the beauty of the Colorado River, the high country basin, into Arapaho National Forest, and the climb up 9,534 foot Ute Pass.

The sausage didn't complain when we popped into the National Forest office for a map of the area. Detailed maps are always a cyclists' friend. Though the Adventure Cycling maps were fine, we found we liked different perspectives on where we were. Also, we carried state maps to get a broader look at the places.

The sausage didn't say anything when we met up with Roger and Kathy again. It's always a reality check traveling with other riders, giving you a chance to see how your touring style fares against others. We had trailers. They had saddlebags. We were from the East. They were from the West. We carried too much stuff. They didn't. We had a frozen sausage. They didn't.

Jimmy Dean was with Jan as we climbed Ute Pass. About three miles from the top, the mercury took a dip and the afternoon rain fell in the form of hail, providing us with a thin white coating that soon melted away, like Mr. Dean was doing.

Deciding to call it a day at the top of the pass, we all set up tents and tried to get out of the rain. That evening Jan cooked Jimmy Dean for dinner in a sausage noodle casserole. A most tasty way to dine at the top of Ute Pass, he was shared with Roger and Kathy.

Later during a post-dinner stroll, we happened upon an RV. Knocking on the door for water, as we were dry camping that night,

SUMMIT SAUSAGE CASSEROLE

Ingredients:
1/2 pound of small bow tie pasta
1 12 oz. frozen sausage
1 can cream of mushroom soup
1/2 cup of spreadable soft cheese
Directions:
Cook off sausage and set aside. Boil enough water to cook pasta. Partially drain water from pasta as remaining water will be the equivalent of one can liquid. Add soup and stir in scrambled sausage and soft cheese. The sausage is spicy so no additional seasoning is necessary. The consistency is that of a loose noodle casserole, almost like eating a hearty stew. It is very warming.

we struck up a conservation with the couple inside. They were a man and woman from Arizona who were on their way to Canada. They invited all four of us into their mobile rig for dessert. Hot tea first, then came the homemade plum wine and then triple sec and cookies.

Good thing Jimmy Dean was history. With the six of us in the RV, space was at a premium. Even a defrosted sausage would have been a tight squeeze.

That night on the walk back to the tent, an idea simmered in my head.

There is a quick gear check list that bicyclists can use every day before pedaling. It's called the ABC Check. "A" means to check the air in your tires. "B" stands for inspecting the brakes. "C" is the signal to look over the chain, crank and cables.

After biking with Jan and witnessing the defrosting sausage, I figured we could add the letter "D" and come up with one more check.

"D" means to ask, "Honey, anything to *defrost* today?"

Chapter Sixteen

Frisco to Boreas Pass, Colorado

Old Home Day is a New Hampshire tradition that began in 1899 when Governor Frank Rollins tried to woo back former residents who left the small, rural farm towns. Nowadays, the tradition has spread beyond the Granite State and once a year former residents of small towns go home to see the place they grew up in and thank the stars they were smart enough to leave.

Rolling down the splendor of Ute Pass and into Summit County was a bit like Old Home Day for both Jan and me. For me, it was a chance to pedal some familiar territory like along Lake Dillon and onto Main Street in Frisco, plus to see some people I hadn't seen since the '92 ride.

The place was also a kind of crossroads for people in our lives. Jan has a sister Bernie who lives in Colorado and Frisco was the meeting ground for the two. We knew some people who moved from New Hampshire to Colorado and there they were in Frisco to see us rolling along. So we hung out there for a couple of days to reconnect, reminisce and have people drive us around in the comfort of a motorized vehicle.

With thanks to Yogi Berra, it was deja vu all over again.

Up near 9,500 feet in Ute Pass with its stunning backdrop of the jagged Gore Range, a sign proclaimed the county as Colorado's

94

playground.

This may be true. Within the county are some 50 miles of paved bike paths which allow riders to pedal among the towns of Silverthorne, Dillon, Frisco and Breckenridge. Link it up with the paths in neighboring Eagle County and ride to Vail and Aspen. The Colorado Trail runs through it, while fly-fishermen cast their luck for trout in the cold streams at over 9,000 feet. In winter, skiers and snowboarders play on the runs at Breckenridge, Copper, Keystone and Arapaho Basin.

We wound down Ute Pass and turned onto Route 9's narrow shoulder and found Summit County experiencing boom times. The construction began outside Silverthorne's sprawl where the road was being widened and more homes were being constructed in a golfing community.

Not only was the road torn up, so were the bike paths. The paths near the Silverthorne/Dillon line were moved as new traffic lights had been put in.

Instead of chirping birds, the chirps were of construction trucks backing up. Perhaps Summit County could be the site of a film called "A Condo Runs Through It."

Such is summer life in a ski town.

Once the madness of Dillon was left behind, the bike path around the reservoir came into view and with it the memories of six years earlier when I was cycling through and met Mark Fox and John Fayhee. Both

Colorado's terrain was rugged and beautiful.

95

worked for the daily paper in Frisco. Back in '92, Fox snapped the photos while Fayhee did the interview for a story about my ride that appeared in the *Summit County Daily News*. One of the photos Fox took was later used on the cover of my first book, *Against the Wind*.

Both were still in Frisco.

Fox was busy, but did have time for a chat. Fayhee, who had penned several books and contributed to "Backpacker" magazine, met us later for a beer and the next day for breakfast. We discussed various adventures, ski town life and other sundry items. It's nice to know that some relationships can begin right where they left off.

After meeting them, it seemed the whole world was passing through our Pine Cove campsite in the Peninsula Recreation Area on the shores of Lake Dillon.

First came Brian Webster and a buddy of his, complete with 12 pack which was quickly consumed. Jan and I knew Webster, a television cameraman, because he had worked at the Resort Sports Network station in North Conway. He had recently left New Hamphsire and taken an assignment with the RSN station in Dillon.

We got around the area quickly because of Jan's sister, Bernie Connell, who showed up at the site soon after Webster. Jan got another family infusion and helped Bernie set up a tent while we boys drank beer. A family visit is always a good morale boost for Jan. She got a chance to catch up on news and be re-energized. Bernie also brought some vegetables from her home garden - tomatoes and herbs - which later made it into Jan's cooking once we left the area.

Having access to wheels, it wasn't a problem that the campground didn't have showers. Bernie, Jan and I went to Webster's cramped one bedroom condominium to get clean and do laundry the next day. He also gave a go at trying to fix my digital camcorder. I had managed to scratch the lens and was not too happy. The scratch remained. I was out of luck.

One of the more interesting interviews was done from a campground pay phone that day during a "live chat" on the ABC

News web site. With us in Colorado and a producer on the phone in Seattle, we fielded questions for about 45 minutes from people all over the world in countries from Sweden to Venezuela. There was even a question from down the road in Silverthorne. The day before we had been allowed to use the town offices to e-mail a story.

People e-mailed the questions in, the producer read them to us on the phone and she would type in the response.

Another Granite State ex-patriot materialized as well. Though many invitations had gone out to people over the miles to join us on our ride, there was only one taker - Tim Sparns. Former ski patroller at Wildcat and Black Mountains in New Hampshire, Sparns moved to the Denver area where he worked as a manager for a food company. He drove to Frisco that Friday in August and showed up at our campsite with a bottle of white wine and four plastic glasses. This was excellent, considering lunch was at the Backcountry Brewery in Frisco with Fayhee over a pitcher of wheat beer. Tim, Bernie, Jan and I later met for dinner at Golden Annie's and enjoyed the Mexican fare along with a few well-earned margaritas.

There were no hangovers on Saturday morning, the day we were to leave Frisco. Webster had arranged for us to be interviewed on television.

So Bernie gave us a lift into Dillon for a 7:30 a.m. live interview on KRSN-TV. Jan was a bit nervous but handled herself well, having grown accustomed to answering questions about the ride every day from people we met. The TV gig went quickly and it was back to the campground to pack up and move out for the next Rocky Mountain climb.

On this day Sparns was to ride with us during the long and steady climb up Boreas Pass at 11,482 feet.

But we needed breakfast first and it was a good one as Bernie and Fayhee met us at 10:30 a.m. at the Sagebrush Cafe in Breckenridge. Sparns, Jan and I left the campground for the bike path along the lodgepole pines and the 12 miles to a busy Breckenridge for breakfast.

Good-byes are always hard (and some tearful) and we had two that day, the first to Bernie and Fayhee, and later to Sparns.

The above treeline climb up Boreas Pass Road is one of those routes that the tourists tackle. Once a railroad bed for the Denver South Park and Pacific Railroad, the pass was one of the easiest crossings of the Continental Divide - number 15 - thus far. Throw fifty pounds in a trailer behind you and the hill's a bit more of a challenge.

Having Tim ride with us was a welcome change of pace and the Rockies were were in their glory that day.

There were even a few human sideshows to keep us laughing. One guy in a pickup truck with Montana plates was walking his dog. He was driving slowly and his black and white dog was running behind!

Another goofy event was watching five guys with beers at a cut-off hit golf balls into the national forest!

At the summit, we watched in disbelief as a cyclist got off his bike, reached in his bag for cigarettes, lit one up and then boasted he just cycled to the top.

But the best thing I saw at the top of the climb was Jan celebrating. There, she jumped up and down and screamed to Boreas, the God of the North Wind, "I did it. I did it." This was the first pass she didn't walk. She rode the whole way.

She had a smile that didn't go away. Not when Tim said good-bye and not on the other side of the pass when we really could have used his, or any of the Old Home Day crowd's help.

Chapter Seventeen

Boreas Pass to Marshall Pass, Colorado

I was sitting at the top of Boreas Pass, under the sign, when I first noticed the problem.

I didn't say anything. Jan was beaming. Tim and strangers were taking pictures.

Denial was my solution.

The trailer was cracked.

This was not a good thing.

Actually, I didn't even notice the thin crack in the fork of the rig that attached to the rear axle until someone else pointed it out. Initially, I had hoped this was nothing more than paint chipping away.

The smart thing would have been to act immediately, given that we had a bunch of Summit County buddies with a wealth of information, contacts, and motorized vehicles.

The dumb thing was to deny the problem and ride on hoping that it wouldn't get worse.

Starting down over Boreas Pass meant a return to nothingness. We were riding from cappuccino to black coffee, from paved bike paths to rough and rugged trails, from the lush of the pines back into the vastness and raw beauty of the high desert, and smack into potential trouble which could not be fixed with incantations, incense, or duct tape. What problem could a little hairline fracture be anyway?

That evening we camped about eight miles from the top of the pass, down in the comfort of willows. Nearby was a creek where a fly-fisherman was painting the sky with a splendid arc. A simple ten to two motion produces such poetry in the out of doors.

As we dined on orzo with fresh tomato, squash (after you've hauled frozen sausage, you'll carry nearly anything), garlic, basil, and salmon provided by Jan's sister Bernie, it was time to confess to Jan about the crack in the trailer fork. Jan took the news in stride, taking a look at the potential disaster in waiting, and agreeing that it was no paint chip.

There was nothing to do but ride on because we were in the middle of nowhere. Keep an eye on it. If it got worse, click our hiking boots together three times and say, "crack be gone." Worst case, we could wrap it in duct tape, a backwoods placebo.

Nowhere is relative. Somewhere is a place that has the things you need. Nowhere is a place that doesn't have the things you need.

In Como, somewhere between nowhere and somewhere, we found the Como Depot B&B, a neat old inn, that was open on Sunday (the store in town wasn't open until 10 a.m. and we were on an early riding rampage) that served up hearty Mexican eggs which amounted to refried beans, green chilies, fried eggs, cheddar cheese, hash browns, and a corn tortilla. This didn't fix the trailer, but it certainly filled our stomachs.

From Como, we wound through the high desert monotony of South Park, seeing rolling hills and grazing domestic buffalo. During this soporific stretch, Jan noticed my trailer wheel wobbling. Upon further investigation, we saw the rear axle was bent and the ball bearings of the wheel were exposed.

It wasn't until the thriving community of Hartsel (population 111) we found not only a convenience store but a working pay telephone to call the trailer manufacturer in California and ask for help. Even on a Sunday, they answered our S.O.S.

It was decided on Monday, they would send a new fork, rear

axle and wheel to a bike shop in Salida, about 50 miles away. In the interim, they suggested massive amounts of duct tape be wrapped around the crack and ride the smoothest surfaces to Salida.

It was a lot of bumpy, washboard roads, and a lot of worry.

Nothing taxes the mind more than potential impending doom. Matters were not helped that there was a whole lot of nothing until Salida. That night we did some bootleg camping with no water source which meant we were loaded up on water so the heavier the load, the more the trailer would wobble.

The trailer snaked. That wasn't a good sign because Jan hates snakes. It is the one life form on this planet she can not say a good word about. Grizzly country was nothing for Jan compared to her fear of snakes. Even harmless snakes we come across while hiking in the White Mountains of home can make her run scared straight behind me, placing me as the shield between her and slinky Sam.

We had seen snakes on the trip. If Jan has to see a snake, her preference is roadkill.

Being somewhat out of our element, we thought every snake we saw would be a poisonous rattler ready for its death strike as we cycled by, much like every bear we never saw would be a grizzly poised to sink its sharp death into our tenderloins. There were times we would ride along the road, and quickly pass a snake. It would not be in my best interest if I asked her if she had seen a snake. Out of sight, out of mind.

After 45 miles of wobbling and worry, we were dry camping somewhere off a subdivision road where house lots waited for houses. It was one of those rare times on the Great Divide Route when public land wasn't around for our sleeping pleasure and we just kind of decided to camp over there.

There were two requirements: no rocks and no snakes. Rocks under a tent become rocks under a sleeping pad which evolve into rocks under a sleeping bag which turn into a pain in the neck and back.

Snakes are another story. When Jan fears there are snakes around, she does her snake dance. Somewhere along the line she heard that snakes are sensitive to the vibrations of the ground, which tells them mountain bikers are near and they would go away. So, she would do her snake stomp around the tent to send the word out to the reptile crew that Jan was in the house and don't you mess with her. This sight would be particularly memorable if Jan had to, say, use the restroom. There were times the restroom was just over there. So there would be Jan, doing her outdoor version of "Stomp" before assuming the position.

That would be the most improper time to yell something like "car," which both of us would do when the other was in the middle of relief.

To this day, this works surprisingly well, even on hiking trails.

More often than not, the car never materializes. That night we didn't see snakes either, and the rocks weren't a problem. There was only the rain, thunder, and lightening as dreams of ball bearings, cracked forks, and duct tape danced through the night.

Monday morning brought hope and Salida. I couldn't help but be optimistic leaving the tundra-like wasteland and seeing the massive Sawatch Range and its 14,000 foot Collegiate Peaks with its Ivy League names of Harvard, Columbia, Yale, and Princeton. Green returned by the Arkansas River as we neared Salida. Finally, we were somewhere again. With a population of nearly 5,000 people, the town had fairly inexpensive motels, restaurants, a funky downtown area with lots of red brick buildings, southwestern flair, and of course, a bike shop.

The owner at the Otero Bike Shop on F Street said he had spoken to the guy from B.O.B. (the trailer people) and the parts were on the way by overnight mail.

Soon the wobble worries would be over.

On the same day that President Clinton admitted to the public he had mislead them about his relationship with intern Monica Lewinsky, we rolled through town, found a motel and set up shop. Showers, computer stuff, it was all part of the rest of the day. There was nothing to do but relax because in the morning, all our problems would be gone.

But they weren't.

Apparently in this part of the world overnight mail takes two nights. Optimism was squashed when we saw the man in brown delivering goods around town and asked him if he had any packages for the bike shop that day.

Nope. Probably tomorrow, he said, Wednesday, in the late afternoon.

Down but not out, we checked out of one hotel to move to another, next to the shipping company. This waiting for parts, in Salida and back at the beginning in Whitefish, had cost us about a week's worth of travel time, not to mention expenses like food, lodging and alcohol to assuage the worry associated with the waiting.

Not-Another-Pass-Again-Pasta

Ingredients:
1 pound angel hair pasta
2 ounces sun dried tomatoes
1 can anchovy filets
1/3 cup olive oil
2 tablespoons garlic flakes
1/2 cup asiago cheese

Directions:
Have all ingredients ready as this dish cooks quickly. Slice sun dried tomatoes into 1/8 inch strips. Boil enough water to cook angel hair. In pan lid, heat olive oil and immediately add the tomatoes, garlic flakes and anchovies. The anchovies will break up while heating. When pasta is cooked, drain, then toss in oil mixture. If available, top with freshly grated asiago cheese.

Jan whittled away the time by sewing. She found a sewing machine at the motel. We were doing some product testing along the way and Jan had received a sleeveless bicycle shirt that was mailed to her in Silverthorne. It was too big. She spotted the sewing machine, asked if she could use it and hemmed away to make the green-blue top fit.

While bobbing about in town latter that day, a green and white van stopped alongside us and a bearded man rolled down his window. He had seen us around town with our trailers and wondered if we were doing the Divide.

That's how we met Tom Anderson, a Florida-based artist who also had done some bike touring in Europe, Colorado and

Washington state. That night he showed up at our motel and we all went to an all-you-can-eat chicken dinner to talk biking. Anderson, a painter for some 21 years, was traveling between art shows in a former church van, carrying all he needed with him from paints, brushes, and shrink wrap to his creations and hardware needed to hang his work at the shows. His next one was in Evergreen, north of Salida and west of Denver.

His wife and daughter were back east and he picked our brains about the route. He wasn't looking to do the whole thing, but a section.

We moved in with Anderson the next day, leaving the hotel to share a campsite with him.

Instead of pacing the campground like caged tigers on Wednesday waiting for late afternoon to arrive, Jan and I opted to ride on a bit.

We turned into slackpackers.

John Fayhee would be proud. He's the writer I had met in '92 and again a few days before in Frisco. A big time backpacker, he would go on these epic hikes, but from time to time would use friends or serendipitous encounters with others to have his full backpack ferried ahead. His argument was simple: you're still hiking. Who cares if it's with a heavy load or not.

In 1992, Fayhee had offered to ferry my gear ahead to give me a break getting out of Frisco. He also marveled that I rode in hiking boots. The same offer was made this time around and both Jan and I, both in hiking boots, politely turned him down, being stalwart mountain bikers who could carry everything.

That was then.

We both needed to get out on the trail again instead of letting our blood pressures boil again. So with Anderson having a van, it was our ticket to ride. Then once the parts came, he would drive us to where we stopped and we could continue on.

So Jan and I pedaled some 12 gear-free miles to the base of Marshall Pass. If you've ever had a broken arm and then marveled at how light your arm felt after the cast was removed, that's what it was like to ride without lugging 50 pounds of stuff. Though we doubted it, maybe Anderson would have liked to bag his art schtick and carry our stuff to Mexico. He certainly wouldn't starve with us. Those DiSisto girls from that Massachusetts high school were on to something. Carrying stuff is for mules.

Our fantasy was short-lived as we zipped back into town and the campground where Anderson was wrapping his art in plastic shrink wrap for the show on a picnic table. It was like a huge cylinder of Handiwrap.

In shorts, t-shirt and baseball cap, he went to work wrapping his paintings.

"Meeting you guys is just a wonderful thing," he said. "You're the only people I've met who are doing it. You can read it in the magazine and see the pictures, but it's much better to really talk to somebody."

I wanted to talk to the guy at the bike shop. Around 5 p.m., I called. The parts were in. So we got into Tom's van and he drove us to the bike shop where the fork awaited.

Back at the campground, the new fork was fitted to the trailer, we all consumed a glorious pasta and beer dinner and for the third straight night, Jan and I were able to take showers.

It was a clean beginning before returning to the dirt of the Divide and the long, gentle climb up Marshall Pass with its shaded aspen groves and startled deer who must have marveled at that brand, spanking new fork.

Chapter Eighteen

Marshall Pass, Colorado to the New Mexico border

The 154 mile stretch between Salida and Del Norte was a pretty lonely piece of high country real estate. The raspberries were ripe on the downside of Marshall Pass, plump enough to put on the brakes for a little nosh down the notch. Wildlife outnumbered people though there were ranchers and day mountain bikers about. Simple wooden fences were part of the wide and windy landscape along with elk, fox, rabbits, and a big old lovable black mutt that followed us for a spell. Mailboxes meant there were people, but isolation seemed to be the address.

Dry creek beds were reminders to fill up on water whenever we could. There was nothing to do - and hope for another Montana Charlie's that never materialized - but ride through the Gunnison and Rio Grande National Forests going from the La Garita Mountains to the San Luis Valley during some 50 mile days of pedaling.

Up and over Cochetopa Pass, we crested Divide crossing seventeen. The eyes of the aspens, so reminiscent of the birch trees back home, followed us as we danced with 10,000 feet. Elevation hadn't been a problem. We were going slowly, not flying to Denver and then driving to a ski area for a dizzying day of getting used to the elevation. Acclimating was easy.

We cycled over Carnero Pass near some of the most stunning rock column formations of the entire route. Though Colorado is thought of as ski country, it is also a desert state. There is cactus, red rock, pinion, and juniper.

Sun, clouds, and drizzle were our companions. The solitude was welcome, but so was the decent into Del Norte, with population and restaurants again like an all-you-can-eat-pizza place. A chat in a sporting goods store led us to camping in a downtown park and, after another exhausting day, we settled in for some sleep.

A few hours later, around 3:15 a.m., the assault began and so did our troubles that would last until nearly the New Mexican border.

The deluge came without warning. Instead of Mother Nature's wrath, it was a surge from the park's automatic sprinkler system.

A rapid machine gun fire of water pelted the tent, the bikes, and gear left outside. The water jets launched the attack against us wave by wave. Moving back and forth, giving us cruel hope that the lawn watering was over, the sprinklers played with us like a cat with a mouse. We were trapped, drenched at will.

The noise not only kept us awake, but all the dogs in Del Norte.

To compound the problem, Jan needed to go to the bathroom. There was a public restroom in the park. She was able to time her darting to the toilet in between the assault. When she reached the bathroom, she found it locked.

This was not the best way to start the day that would take us from the small, farming community to the mother of all hills along the Great Divide Mountain Bike Route - Indiana Pass.

In about 25 miles, cyclists gain 4,000 feet in elevation. The pass is the highest point on the ride at 11,910 feet. The first 11 miles out of Del Norte is fairly easy, a paved country road through farms and ranches.

Come dirt, the pain begins.

We rode, we walked, we talked, we balked. If Boreas Pass was the easiest of the twenty-nine hills that led up and over the Divide, Indiana Pass was the beast. The most insulting part of it is that for those people riding the entire route, by this time, you are supposed to be in shape. Indiana Pass is a lesson in what being in shape means. The lesson learned that day was simple, excellence is always another step away especially if you have beans for lunch (or ate too much pizza the night before).

We also learned something else. Don't have a refried bean sandwich for lunch when you are conquering the beast. Jet propulsion fuel it isn't. However, it did provide us with an excuse for frequent breaks and to yell "car" a few times.

"A big no no for the future," is how Jan described the non-discriminating aftereffects of a cold refried bean sandwich while ascending.

The climb was long and hard, but it was also a social event. Pickup trucks stopped and its occupants asked if we were okay, offering us water, and always reacting in either awe or pity when they learned from where we had started.

We walked about 12 miles of the pass, helmets in the trailers, baseball caps on our heads to ward against the Colorado sun in the Rio Grande National Forest.

And Jan found a dime. Forever the scavenger, from berries to firewood, Jan has a knack for finding change. She had over the miles accumulated a handful of pennies, even a quarter yet the nickel had remained elusive. As we gained elevation Jan confided she would really like to collect a dollar in change by the end of the trip.

We also started talking about the victory meal, the first dinner we would have when we got home - lobster.

Two months on the road and thoughts of home start trickling into the mind's theater. There are dreams of showers and refrigeration, microwaves and motor vehicles, drawers and closets filled with clothes. On the road, socks are worn three days in a row. A clean shirt means one that has been doused in deodorant for that illusion of clean. Pop into a restaurant bathroom and look deep into that face in the mirror, especially if you haven't seen it for a couple of days. There are changes. The skin is darker. Lines are etched deeper into it. That face that looks back is thinner.

Down the body, tan lines emerge midway down thighs. The back of ones hand has that badge of honor, caused by the opening in the bike glove. Stay in those restrooms longer and use the hot water. Wash your face, your arms. Lift your shirt and use the paper towels as a washcloth for the biker bath. Use another paper towel to erase that thin layer of dust on the legs.

The whole body is thinner. Talk about a great weight reduction plan. Eat what you want, but pedal your butt off. Ride to eat. Eat to ride. That's the best way to reduce what you carry. Lose weight.

Motel rooms take on a new meaning too. Showers are not just for the body, but throw in some quick-drying clothing like fleece, lycra and polypro and you can kick them around on the shower floor as the dirt washes down the drain. Use the phone to call everyone. Recharge the batteries on the computer. Step over two bikes, two trailers and all that gear that's been taken out of the bags and spread all over the table, chair, desk and television. Get naked and look at the two-tone human in the mirror.

Funny. At home, we run into long distance riders near our home who are on their way to the Maine coast to wrap up their cross-country ride. Every once in awhile, I'll turn to Jan after one has gone and say something like, "Do I ever look like that?" Or "Do I ever smell like that?"

She just nods her head.

But now we talked about lobster. That's what was on our minds as we continued up the pass. Lobsters, steamers, chilled white wine, lemon wedges, fresh tomatoes with feta, basil, garlic, balsamic vinegar and olive oil would be the first meal once we got back home. Since we would still be lean, at least for a few months, we would have a celebratory dessert of cherry/strawberry cheesecake. We were in the land of beef. Shellfish sounded so good.

Before we dug into the claws, we had to dig into ourselves and after about six hours and 14 miles we were on top of Indiana

Pass just in time for the passing afternoon rain. Though there was no sign for the pass, there was the splendor of the pockets of evergreens, the West's signature wooden fences and the massive hulk of Grayback Mountain. The soft Western light bathed the pass and unleashed a vibrancy in greens, yellows and muted earth tones.

To celebrate this accomplishment, we opted to camp in the altitude, in a sheltered grove of trees just off the road. Jan was surprised when I took out a small bottle of tequila I had purchased in Del Norte. We had learned about desert margaritas from Roger and Cathy, the cycling Colorado couple. Tequila and lemonade it was, a couple of plastic clinks with our mugs and we complemented ourselves on a nice job.

I soon learned in a matter of hours it's not a good thing to mix altitude and tequila, especially after having refried beans for lunch. Jan weathered the internal storm in the stomach better than I and as I drifted off to sleep I hoped the morning would bring relief.

It didn't.

Jan's thin blood might have saved her from a similar fate (plus her policy of moderation when it comes to tequila at about 12,000 feet), but I felt the wrath of stupidity that morning as a general malaise and fogginess shrouded my being.

Nonetheless we prodded on to the ugly cousin of the Rockies - Summitville. Once a thriving mining town of 700 people, it was now an EPA Superfund Site. Discolored creeks and rivers in the area mirrored possible contamination.

"Notice. This Creek May Be Contaminated. Not Suitable For Drinking Water", read one sign, a brown one with white lettering.

From afar, the mountain site looks as if someone carved a cross-section out of a hill. Close up, massive trucks grunt up and down as part of a cleanup operation. Ramshackle cabins stand as a reminder on a hillside of what was once a town with taverns, a school, post office, and a sawmill. Across the road, a sign warned of danger from a hazardous area.

Mining is ironic. Under the earth are the raw materials that make the things we need. Ride a bike. Carry a laptop computer. Take pictures with a camera. Cook food on a metal stove. Rape the land to get the raw materials.

The rumble of heavy machinery cut through the silence. The earth shook as a caravan moved by.

The earth was to shake again. Leaving Summitville through the alpine meadows and forests of the Rio Grande National Forest, a massive late morning thunderstorm moved in about five miles outside of Platoro. Thunder echoed through the canyons as we plodded up Stunner Pass. The temperature dipped, the rains burst forth. We were drenched.

I had not been having a good day. Lethargic was the word of the day. Twenty-six miles was the goal, but it was in slow motion. Jan would constantly be waiting for me. Asking me if I was okay, I would nod my head. Then in the darkness of a thunder boomer I stopped.

Straddling the bike in the rain, the bullet like drops ricocheting off my shell, I just looked up into the sky.

Jan stopped.

"Why are you stopping?," she cried against the rain drops.

"Huh," was the response.

Jan wanted to flag down a vehicle. Pickup trucks had their lights on and from time to time one would pass us by, joining in the mud free-for-all that covered us.

"No ride," I said.

Before we took off on the trip, we had agreed we would not accept a ride on this trip. We would do this under our own steam. No matter how miserable, no matter how delirious, no matter what.

A pickup truck, coming right at us, slowed down and stopped. The driver, in glasses and a mustache, rolled down the window. Jan approached.

In the deluge, our bikes, trailers, and wet selves were loaded into the relative cramped comfort of a pickup truck that then turned around on the narrow dirt road so the driver, and his son, could head back to where they had just some from.

Four across in the pickup, the two strangers in the truck just traded comfort for pools of slop on the front seat of the truck.

The driver asked Jan if we had a place to stay in Platoro, the next town. She told him no, but we would look into staying at a lodge there. His reply was that he would take us to the best place in Platoro.

A couple of miles later, we were in a one-room cabin in the remote southern San Juans with an elevation of about 9,750. There was electricity, propane, a wood stove and antlers. The outhouse didn't smell. There was running water that we would have to run to get, huge jugs that needed to be filled.

It had things we desperately needed - warmth and dryness.

All this came courtesy of Charlie Blickhahn, and his son, Charlie Blickhahn.

Father and son had been up for the weekend doing some trout fishing. The two lived in Alamosa. They were on their way home when our paths crossed.

The elder Charlie gave us a quick tour, demonstrating how to operate the stove, turn the electricity on and off, and where to get the water.

All he asked was that we close things up and send him a postcard when we finished the trip.

Then the Charlies left.

The rains didn't. The rain pounded against the cabin, our gear spread all over the room and on the furniture to dry. Jan made tea and I entered dreamland.

It was no dream that rain kept pelting the wooden steps outside the uninsulated cabin and the small boat with motor. Pots and pans were placed on the porch to collect the water so we wouldn't have to make a water run immediately.

The rains did abate. Sleep, rest and a lower elevation did wonders as we took stock of where we were: a cabin with antlers and a big blue happy face on the outside.

Just down the dirt road, past the other weather beaten cabins in this once thriving mining town, was the Skyline Lodge with showers, laundry and the best burgers this side of Summitville. We hadn't showered for five days so once we dried up, it was decided to spend the next night at the lodge with its horns, hides, and heads on the wall.

We even found a bathroom scale in one of the rooms. Jan had dropped about 15 pounds. I had lost about 20. Now that's a weight loss program.

The town, we were told, wasn't plowed in winter and snow often reaches high up to the roofs of the homes. The Conejos River runs through the community and its network of dirt roads. Walk among them and see a lone volleyball

The Divide led from Colorado into New Mexico.

net in a grassy field surrounded by cabins. Red roofs, green roofs, white roofs, propane tanks and utility poles make up the manmade landscape. Meet a couple of other bikers, Matt and Tim from Virginia, who were also doing the Divide. Dogs bark, pickup trucks crawl slowly through the puddles, wood is neatly stacked under the gray skies that always seem to forecast boom and doom.

Indoor plumbing was wonderful and so was awakening to the smell of bacon, walking downstairs and having breakfast.

Platoro, a special place in the middle of nowhere, was a fine town to recharge our biological batteries before heading out for our last day cycling Colorado. Four frozen trout were in tow, defrosting for that night's meal.

The fish were compliments of a most kind father and son.

•••

Low clouds clung close to the pockmarked dirt road leading

out of Platoro. Leaving the comforts of the indoors was becoming a bit harder each time as we rolled through the puddles in the gray morning, following the Conejos River closer to the border of New Mexico, some 40 or so miles away. Clean sometimes lasts a second on the trail as flying mud always leaves its mark on tires, calves, backs, and bags.

By the banks of the river was a tent and two bikes. They belonged to Matt and Tim, the pair of twenty-something cycling vegetarians we had met. Scruffy beard on one, rastafarian hair on the other, they were just starting to crawl out of their quarters when we pedaled by in the chill of the early morning. We waved.

The morning fog lifted. The wetness and muck of the road turned boots and socks wet.

But the sun returned, the sky brightened to blue and dirt was left for the relative dryness of paved Route 17. Near noon, a familiar white and green van appeared by the roadside putting smiles on our faces. Once again, paths crossed and Tom Anderson, the artist we had met in Salida, happened to be passing through the same area we were.

Over lunch at Little Joe's Chuckwagon Cafe, Anderson peppered us with questions about the ride, hearing tales from the sprinkler assault in Del Norte, the Indiana Pass tequila incident and the one-room cabin in Platoro. Too quickly, lunch was over, good-byes were said, and the long six mile climb up La Manga Pass to 10,230 feet began.

A big lunch and a mountain pass is not a good combination. So it's best to walk, let the digestive juices do their thing and take two hours to get to the top.

Every once in awhile the maps we were using would goof, whether it be directions, mileage or description of the terrain. This time it was mileage for a turn, about five miles off.

But still we managed to find the right dirt road that led to a railroad crossing.

It would be nice to say that we saw a plume of smoke and heard the grunting of gears as a taste of the Old West passed right before our eyes taking passengers through the tunnels and over the trestles in the high alpine landscape between the states of Colorado and New Mexico.

We did not see the black locomotive of the Cumbres and Toltec railroad during its 64 mile run that day. The narrow gauge tracks cross between the two states seven times during the journey.

We did see Matt and Tim, again. Though a bit more of one than we would have liked to see.

There is a fence and cattle guard that stands between Colorado and New Mexico. There isn't a welcome center in these parts, but a brown sign that informs those who pass they are entering both Carson National Forest and New Mexico. It's a fine place to take a picture, rest a bit, and make a decision that the first place we see that looks like a good place to camp is home for the night. After all, there was ample wood to collect for a fire and the trout was probably defrosted by this time.

It's also where we saw a couple of yellow jerseys rolling our way on mountain bikes with saddle bags. Matt and Tim were about to enter the fifth and final state of their Great Divide journey as well.

Long distance bicyclists are an unusual breed and we were about to see something that Ray Stevens could have incorporated into his song "The Streak."

Before I could yell, "Look out Ethel," Matt was getting off his bike and changing the position of his riding shorts. Instead of covering his genitals like they were made to do, he was wearing them on his head. Who are we to judge the

Smoking the Rainbow

Ingredients:
Freshly caught trout
Tarragon vinegar
Tin foil

Directions:
Wrap each trout individually in foil like a Tootsie Roll. Place on blazing campfire and turn each trout every few minutes. If it is a direct flame, the trout will be done in ten minutes. If the trout is on a grill, it will take a bit longer. Open foil. Skin will stick to foil. Pull out center bone and season with vinegar. Finger licking good.

customs of others? At every Divide crossing, Jan and I did our kiss, hug, helmet thing. So if a guy wanted to get naked from the waist down and pedal his way across the border to New Mexico with his cycling shorts on his head, who are we to say he's nuttier than a fistful of cashews?

There was nothing to do but feel sorry for Tim and take a picture of Matt's New Mexico border crossing to keep under lock and key until Matt decides to run for president some day.

Thankfully, when he entered New Mexico he returned to normal or at least he put his pants back on.

"Don't even think about it," said Jan as I shot her a mischievous look that only she could interpret as meaning she or we should enter the annals of Co-ed Naked Great Divide Mountain Biking.

A spot to camp was quickly found at the top of hill. Our tent was a fine place to ride out the afternoon rains.

That evening, the four of us camped together, two vegetarians and two carnivores. By the campfire, four defrosted trout sprinkled with tarragon vinegar and rolled in tin foil cooked as I fired up the stove for some rice. Matt and Tim were working on pasta, peas and curry. Under the New Mexican sky, the land of yellow license plates and the Land of Enchantment, we shared our meals and a day of naked truth.

Chapter Nineteen

Carson National Forest to outside Vallecitos, New Mexico

Forget the Land of Enchantment. Though rich in heritage and diverse in culture, the yellow license plate state provided a rocky reception for riders. Steep and dusty was more like it. Hang on for the bumps. Rattle the nerves and rattle the chains. Walk those downhills instead of steering over a stone and slipping.

After Montana, it's New Mexico that has the most miles of a state on the Great Divide Mountain Bike Route. On paper it's 678 miles of ups and downs from the high country of the north along the Brazos Ridge which overlooks the expanse of the Cruces Basin Wilderness to the cactus of the Chihuahuan desert in the south with its elusive shade.

Try out your high school Spanish. Go into a restaurant and have both green and red bottles of Tabasco sauce on the table. Look out on the badlands of geologic nothingness or put your face right up to a ponderosa pine and smell butterscotch. It was all waiting for us once we crossed into New Mexico, experiencing that trail giddiness that comes with reaching the next phase of a journey.

Four states down. One to go.

Broken rocks seemed to comprise the base of New Mexico's forest service roads. The true Continental Divide lay to the west of us and it would be a few miles before we crossed it again. That didn't mean there weren't any hills because there is always a hill. In New Mexico they were tough going up and tough going down. A sign saying "Primitive Road Unsuited For Public Use" didn't put a smile on our faces either.

Adding to the strain was the load. Water was getting scarce again. Streams that were supposed to be flowing, or at least trickling, weren't. The handful that were looked unappetizing. Still we would stop, pump and carry water, more so than we would have liked, but enough to lessen the fears that we run out.

The same was true about food. What we had is what there would be for the first 68 miles of New Mexico. That is when the first food source would be available. On the map, it was the small town of Canon Plaza and the establishment was described as "Snack stand on left may be open." I was thinking hot dog. Two-fifty each. No problem. Dangle a hot dog in front of me while on a bike trip and I'll ride for miles. After Canon Plaza the route wound through Vallecitos, but the map said there were no services. The first real grocery store in New Mexico, according to the map, was El Rito, some 90 miles from the Colorado border.

If we wanted it, we were carrying it, and maybe adding another 10 or so pounds each for the butt-busting boogie.

Though it was no store, Jan was marveled by a wooden teepee high on a ridge under the bright blue sky. Almost as towering as a handful of the sparse evergreens, the teepee could have been hidden to those keeping their eyes to the ground. Not to Jan. She was riding with her head high that mile and wanted to stop.

A simple wooden structure like many I had seen up in Arctic Scandinavia, it was a fine place to weather out the rain. An unexpected stop, an unexpected place, it became a symbol for her.

"Did you see the teepee?," Jan asked Tim and Matt who finally caught up to us that day, opting not to start riding before eight a.m. like we did. Young knees and young lungs can do that you know.

Neither had and then they were off, putting on more miles than we would. It was just a bunch of stripped down logs leaning against each other. Just as hikers will travel the Appalachian Trail or the Pacific Crest Trail, those of the two-wheel set can pedal up and down the same route and see different things, meet different people, have different experiences often even within minutes of each other.

A deer darts across the road. Some see it, others don't. Scattered thunder boomers drench one side of the road and not the other.

Then there was the rancher who stopped by Jan as she was tinkering with her rear axle, bending it back due to the strain on the trailer from the tortuous route. He fired away with questions. Where are you going? Where are you from? How many miles do you go every day? Jan rattled off the answers like a pro. After every one, the rancher would say, "Bless your little heart."

That little heart was really quite big, and it needed a rest, and a fire. So after 40 miles and the first full day of cycling in New Mexico, we decided to dry camp about a half mile from a sign saying Cisneros Park. Snow still hung on to the peaks of southern Colorado, the wind fluttered the leaves of the aspens and that glowing beautifully hued, southwestern sunset worked its' magic.

What a wonderful way, despite the hardships, to end a "Bupkis Day."

Bupkis, and there are a few different ways to spell it, is a Yiddish word meaning "nothing." If there was a day when we spent no money it would be a "Bupkis Day." It can be fairly easy to have a Bupkis Day when you're on a bike. Stock up at night, roll out the next morning, just eat what you've got and camp over there. Badda bing - you spent bupkis!

We had our share of Bupkis Days on the ride so far. Day two, crossing the Whitefish Divide in northern Montana, was a Bupkis Day. We hit a couple of Bupkis Days the first week of July in Montana too. In Wyoming, we belted out a Double Bupkis while crossing the Great Divide Basin. I mean, if there's no place to spend your money, it's got bupkis potential.

The remoteness of New Mexico was prime territory for hitting Double Bupkisses. But always in the back of mind was the elusive Triple Bupkis. I had tried and tried to pull off the Triple. After two days of eating only what you had, there was always that convenience store that seemed to pop up, that gas station soda machine with its chilled cans that rivaled day-old warm water being carried in a bottle. Bupkis be damned. I would look in my handlebar bag for every coin possible to feed a soda machine after two days in the sweltering sun. Willpower? Not exactly. I had tried but the great Triple just seemed to be out of my reach.

Could we be cycling through the Land of the Enchanted Triple Bupkis?

Probably not, as I had those hot dogs on my mind as we started a new day which turned out to have more of the same: steep climbs, sharp and massive rocks, stunning basin vistas.

Then there were cows with attitude. They just wouldn't budge. "Move it on over," by Hank Williams and made famous by George Thorogood was on my mind as I yelled "moooooove" to the cattle. They paid me no mind. We would stop. They would eventually go on their way or we would pretend we were on a slalom ski race course and go between them, albeit slowly. They were not impressed with our dexterity either.

If it weren't cows, then it was a climb, like the five mile grunt up to Hopewell Lake. Gradual at times, there were also some surprises. Our trusty maps had elevation profiles as well. We always checked them before heading out. At times, they weren't always accurate. That usually meant there was more uphill than expected, like up to the lake. On the plus side, the maps also would point out vistas. Zipping down Burned Mountain with its far-reaching basins, the beauty was always better than the written word on the map.

Not only was the route tough on mountain bikers, it also proved an obstacle to cars. We stumbled across a car with two young women and an infant inside. They were stuck in the ruts. With not too much clearance under the car, they needed some assistance.

We were heading in the direction they there coming from and told us of a house we were going to pass. Please tell the guy there they were stuck so he would come to help them, one said.

A few miles later, there was the house. The yard was gated. The gate was locked. We didn't see a doorbell. So there stood Jan, off her bike, yelling hello to anyone who might be inside. Maybe it took a minute, but a life form did materialize through the door of the house and to the gate. It was an old man. He and Jan exchanged pleasantries. She told him about the car, the occupants and the problem. He would go get them. Jan Duprey became rural mountain bike messenger: signed, sealed and delivered.

Seven miles later we came to the first store in New Mexico along the Divide. There were no hot dogs, no hamburgers either. I couldn't get a slice of pizza, no nachos. Cold beer? Forget about it.

As luck would have it, the Summer Store was open.

The owner had just gotten out of school.

His name was Joe and he was a high school student. Usually the store would open around 4:20 p.m. when he got home from school. But on this day, it was 2:30 p.m. and we were the first customers.

Describing the store or snack shack is simple. Think Sears. Think about that small corrugated metal shack you can throw in the backyard to toss in the tools, bikes, sleds, nuts, bolts and fishing rods. That was the Summer Store. Picture a few hubcaps against a white fence with white painted rocks under a white sign with blue lettering that said, "Summer Store." Imagine a huge inverted spool, like one used for cable, as a table. Inside the store was cold soda, snacks, candy, fishing hooks, and worms for sale, but no hot dogs. We did devour pastry, candy, cold soda and chips, and had seconds on everything. Bupkis be damned.

Before you knew it, another customer dropped in. She was a photographer, working on a coffee table book about mom and pop stores in New Mexico. Taking pictures in black and white, she explained what she was doing to Joe who didn't mind that she took photos. Jan and I were even in a few, a couple of model mountain bikers.

121

After the rest and the photo shoot - we never did see a finished product - it was back to the ruts and sharp rocks, passing through the next town, Vallecitos, which was little more than a blip. Once again, it looked like heavy rains for the afternoon as the sky quickly darkened about four miles later. Somewhere near 8,000 foot high Valle Grand Peak, there was a cattle guard that was crossed. Jan had the foresight to say, "Let's put up a tent there so we don't get caught in the rain."

Quickly, as the thunder roared across the sky, we had the tent up, moved inside and listened to the heavy rain outside. We dozed a bit and awoke to a swamp inside the tent. In our desire to escape the rains, we set up in a depression that became a puddle. So when the rains stopped, we hung the wet stuff outside on the bikes, trees and makeshift bungie cord clothesline, moved the tent so that it was near waterfront property and not in it, and fired up the stove for some hot tea.

I bet super models have better accommodations.

Chapter Twenty

Outside Vallecitos to Santa Fe National Forest, New Mexico

New Mexico's middle finger was held firmly in front of our faces as we started the day miserably damp. Wet, muddy, and seeking a restaurant or grocery store, we eventually left the slippery, rutted Forest Route 44 for a return to blessed pavement in El Rito.

Adobe-style homes - even the post office - were everywhere. At 10 a.m., the only thing open was Martin's grocery store. The white face building with green trim listed El Rito's elevation at 6,870. The town also housed a ranger district office, closed of course. We found shade and it was in the cool comfort that we wolfed down the rolls, corned beef and fruit juices we had purchased at the grocery store where we also filled up on water.

Thankfully, the road was an easy ride and when we sought to beat the heat by popping into the Blue Spruce Bar and Package Store for a soda the owner told us about a festival, one honoring a saint, being held in Abiquiu some four miles away.

Up to Abiquiu we rode and entered a courtyard that was a throwback in time.

123

MARTY BASCH

Abiquiu's plaza is a special place, a town square that brings back visions of the Wild West, Mexico, Spain, another time. A sign we saw said respect Abiquiu, don't take any pictures. Park only in designated areas. There were stands selling foods like tacos and burritos. People milled about. It was a joyous day. Jan likened it to a church picnic and we were indeed outside a church, a brown adobe-style (that's the extent of my southwest architecture knowledge) one. Talk about being in the right place at the right time. Hot dogs? No thanks. Tacos and burritos were fine replacements.

We took a tour of the church and even were asked by a priest if we wanted to buy a ticket for the raffle. What was the prize?

"A pig," he responded.

A pig in a blanket maybe, but a pig in a trailer? No thanks was the answer. In hindsight, we should have just bought a ticket anyway, in the spirit of giving that had followed us down the Divide. Had we actually won the pig, I'm sure we could have traded it for a taco or two.

Not only did the Chama Valley community have a church or two (even a monastery), but a mosque, too. A spiritual place, there is a mix of cultures from Spaniards to Native Americans, Catholic to Islam. Once the jumping off place for those riding the 1,200 mile Old Spanish Trail to Los Angeles on mules, it was now a stop for two-wheeled pack-carrying mountain bikers doing the Great Divide.

Abiquiu is also a village rich in artists. Choose a media and there's an artist who will create with it. Clay, jewelry, beads, wood, you name it. Mention painting and there's one who is synonymous with Abiquiu and New Mexico: Georgia O'Keeffe.

A pioneer in modern art, O'Keeffe was born in 1887 in Wisconsin, but later fell in love with and eventually moved to New Mexico. Though there is an entire museum in Santa Fe dedicated to her work, there is also her home and studio in Abiquiu. Now run by the Georgia O'Keeffe Foundation, tours are given to the public by appointment.

But not on this festival day when it was open to everyone for free.

Can't take photos. Couldn't even jot notes. We were among those given a tour of the artist's 5,000 square foot home and studio. In the kitchen were teas and spices. A courtyard, in the adobe-style home, was in the middle. In it was a large garden.

Abiquiu charmed us during the few hours we were there. But the road leading out of it, gentle initially, turned rough and rocky along Abiquiu Creek and steep too, as we climbed up Polvadera Mesa.

Locals who saw us giving our bikes a bath in the creek told us there was a camp site up ahead complete with tables and the creek running by it. The sound of running water was a pleasure to hear, and to have. Out came the wash cloth. We heated the water with the stove. This was pure joy.

That joy was short-lived once we loaded our bottles with water and hit the road again the next morning, starting with a five mile grunt up the Polvadera Mesa. The landscape was changing. Though there had been rain, there had been a sharp drop in the number of creeks for us to draw water from to filter. Cactus was starting to appear. Shade was starting to disappear. Clouds were welcome in the sky, even if they forebode heavy rains. They could block the sun. When the trees were there in the Santa Fe National Forest, we would try to ride in the shade. This wasn't the harsh desert yet, but already we were joking about using a "Get Out of the Desert Free Card" if we happened to stumble upon one. This was not our element.

Black volcanic rocks littered the dirt road and, speaking of litter, portions of New Mexico were just plain dirty. Beer cans, beer bottles, you name it, were thrown by the roadside. Going to the dump in New Mexico meant hauling it from your home into the woods.

We were also going slowly. Fifteen miles took four hours. Lunch would be in the shade of juniper-pinon trees. Water was a constant concern and there wasn't much.

When there wasn't a creek or stock tank or hose, there would be cars. Necessity is the mother invention and it will turn thirsty bikers into traffic cops, stopping cars for a chance that they too would be carrying water.

These weren't cars traveling at 60 miles per hour down the highway, but vehicles going slowly on bumpy dirt roads. Often, they would stop anyway in an attempt to satisfy their curiosity about these trailer-pulling, helmeted, lycra-wearing aliens who apparently hadn't heard about the invention of the engine yet.

One car slowed down as we were resting by the side of the road. As it did, we waved and they came to a stop and we asked if they happened to have any water with them. They didn't, but Therese and Rick from Santa Cruz did have some cans of lemonade and gave us two. They were looking for a particular canyon in the forest and were having trouble finding it. We were of no help. But they suggested they could help us find water. There was room for one of us in the car and it was decided I would go with them, taking our water bottles, and hunt for water. For forty minutes we went up and down dirt roads but found no water. We did find a bunch of people packing up their camp. They had water and filled the bottles. We headed back to Jan who was able to rest, catch up in her diary, write a few postcards and find shade.

Not only that, she found a nickel.

We returned to the world of roadside bottles and cans to schlep ourselves up and over the enchanted steep and rocky landscape. There seemed to be an infusion of pickup trucks with two or three guys abreast cruising the woods.

Even before opening day, hunters were out scouting the canyons, mesas and forests of the Santa Fe National Forest for elk. Deer, elk and birds like grouse could be hunted as September neared.

"Seen any elk?," was the question most asked during our contact with those inside the pickup trucks and SUVs high in the mountains.

As they scanned the woods, looking for signs of game, I heard a sound I didn't want to hear. On riding day 55, after over 1900 miles and four states, the sound finally caught up to me.

Pssssst.

I had a flat, the rear tire.

Fixing a flat isn't all that difficult, especially if you have the right tools. Even a mechanically-challenged guy like me can do it.

The trailer has to be removed. Then the wheel is taken off the bike. A pair of tire irons, these are critical, are then inserted between the rim and tire, and if the planets are all aligned, it's a pretty quick circular motion to separate tire from rim. Take the tube out of the tire.

If you happen to have a spare tube, we did, then replace the punctured one. Put the tube in the tire. Replace the tire on the rim. The wheel goes back on the bike.

Then get the pump and fill it with air.

That was the problem.

No air was going into the tire.

Jan tried it. She couldn't fill the tire either.

All of a sudden carrying one pump between two people was not such a good idea.

It was time for Plan B.

Help.

Jan started to flag down pickup trucks as I feverishly tried to pump up the tire to no avail. Maybe there would be a couple of mountain biking bowhunters who happened to have a pump. The first pickup didn't. Neither did the second. Wasn't it just a couple of miles ago that a couple had given us two cans of lemonade? Help had to arrive.

It was a Sunday. Rodney Martinez from Espanola, his brother and uncle were scouting the forest for elk. It was early evening, on a winding downhill with a little shoulder and the distant thunder was getting louder. There, they were flagged down by Jan.

Martinez is a guide and is used to helping people. He's been stranded during fall snowstorms while hunting, so it was no effort for him to stop to offer assistance.

The trio also tried to pump. They too, couldn't get the tire inflated.

Martinez said he would be by with a portable air compressor in the morning.

He suggested a place for us to camp and about an hour later, stopped by to see if we were okay. We were and we asked if he could take our collapsible jug and bring it back in the morning with water. He said okay.

With our flashlights as the lone source of light, we cooked, we ate. We listened to the thunder and we saw the flashes of lightening. The temperature dropped. The wind picked up.

It could have been a fitful night of sleep, knowing that a tentside air compressor delivery service from Espanola to the east had us on their schedule for first thing in the morning. But what if they didn't come? What if we were out a collapsible jug? We were stranded and dependent upon three strangers in a pickup.

That night a hellacious thunder and lightening storm rocked the tent, shook the ground and turned everything outside the shelter wet. We huddled together, sleeping bag to sleeping bag, seeing each other momentarily during the flashes of light and hoping lightening wouldn't choose our little tent as a landing strip.

In between pockets of sleep, the day dawned chilly and by 7:30, there was Martinez and crew, air compressor, and collapsible jug filled with water. I thought it rude to ask if it wouldn't have been too much trouble to include a couple of cups of coffee, bagels and cream cheese. Then again, Espanola bagels probably weren't up there on the Bagel Top 10 List.

The night's lack of sleep was quickly forgotten and the guys fired up the din of the red air compressor. It was the most pleasant music to start the chilly, wet day.

Except, the tire wasn't filling.

Talk about a deflated ego.

Off came the tire and this time we looked at the tube. There was a hole in it. Wanting to hide somewhere fast, I put in yet another new tube and then got the pump. Maybe it wasn't the pump after all.

Once again, the pump didn't work. It didn't work for the boys or Jan either.

But the compressor was fired up again and this time life was restored to the beaded roll of rubber.

Life was good again. We said thank you and the bowhunters were off in search of elk. We were mobile again and hoping to make it to the town of Cuba about 50 miles away, which hopefully had a bike pump for sale somewhere.

With the advent of hunting season came rolling hunters and their camps. Pickup trucks pulled campers. If there were a clearing, a mini-village sprang up.

It is not necessarily a good thing to be mountain biking in an area where people are hunting. Many times out hiking in the White Mountains of New Hampshire, I've come upon gun-toting hunters in blaze orange. They've been friendly enough, though there is that initial shock of "Hey, he's got a gun and bullets. I've got a pocket knife. Something's not right." Do I feel safe? Yes. Do I like the idea of being in the woods with people with firearms and I don't have any? No.

Hunting season was news to us. There had been no warning from any of the pre-trip literature we read. There was nothing on our maps. We did take solace in the fact it was bowhunting season. I couldn't recall an incident about any bowhunting mishaps.

Then again, somebody's got to be first.

About six hours after we packed up camp and rolled away, a dark and fierce hailstorm turned the pine forest white. The temperature plummeted to near 40.

Jan and I sought shelter in a pine grove as pellets from above ricocheted off the ground. It didn't take long for Jan to start to feel a big chill. Moving while cold is a good way to stay warm. Standing under a bunch of trees and watching as the ground underfoot turns mucky and water starts to rise, is not conducive to comfort.

Jan was shivering, cold, and miserable. I started digging into our bags for everything fleece and helped her out of her cold and clammy clothing and into the soft material so she could stay warm. Even with the fleece and yellow and black shell she had on - no slave to fashion is Jan - she was still a shivering little honeybee.

After about a half hour of life in a pine grove, it was time for Plan B.

129

Help.

The small ravine we had sought shelter in was becoming a river. The steep muddy walls were slick. About 100 yards down the road was a hunter's camp. One trailer had an awning.

Inside, a couple of hunters from the Albuquerque area named Wayne and Jerry were having coffee around the table while Nona was reading a book on the couch.

A knock came from the door.

"Can we stand under your awning?," I asked.

Yes.

Soon, a hand with two towels reached through the door to the awning.

Then, we were invited inside. Jan, the little honeybee, was wrapped in blankets. She was shivering.

"You poor little thing," said Nona, jumping off the couch. "You poor little thing."

We were then pumped with hot coffee and banana-nut muffins.

When the hail had stopped and the sun returned, we all went outside. We set up our tent and spread all our wet, dirty things about the campsite in hopes of drying them out.

We were given beer.

Beer made us very happy.

A fire was started. We brought over some things to dry. We got out the maps and explained our trip.

Dinner time was approaching. We were invited to

Marty and Jan fire up another meal.

eat.

Last year the hunters had killed an elk, named it Bob, and even put pictures of Bob on the refrigerator door. The hunters were having elk burgers and T-bone steak, mashed potatoes, and roasted corn. This was a lot better than the ramen noodles, instant mashed potatoes and tomato paste we carried.

So we dined on elk burgers, or maybe they were Bob burgers, with green chilies wrapped in a flour tortilla.

That night, when it appeared it was going to rain again, Jerry offered us the bedroom in his trailer.

We accepted and slept fitfully with full stomachs and dry clothes. We were safe and dry. In this part of New Mexico, we were thankful for Plan B - Plan Bowhunters.

Chapter Twenty-one

Santa Fe National Forest to outside Grants, New Mexico

Location is everything for the town of Cuba. An odd place with a mishmash of Native American, Anglo and Latino cultures, the town has a population of maybe 1,000 people, and sits by the Jicarilla Reservation, Navajo Reservation and Jemez Pueblo. The Nacimiento Mountains would make for a stunning sunset I would think, if it hadn't been raining the night we were there.

It was the perfect spot to clean up after a mud bath, resupply, not find a bike pump, and head out. It's also something of a crossroads for those on the Great Divide. There is a choice for riders to get to Grants, some 116 miles away. One sticks to dirt, the other is the paved alternative.

I knew which choice Jan was going to vote for since the first hour and a half at the motel was spent cleaning the muck from her bike with a hose while wearing a cotton dress she carried that displayed her biker tan with honor.

She had a mud pie morning. New Mexico's gummy red soil was giving her some trouble. The mud didn't discriminate; both of us needed to pull over, find a stick, and get rid of the muck that was collecting on the tires, brakes, cables and frame.

The relief came when we hit pavement again on Route 126 and the road acted a bit like a washing machine. The rotation of the tires sent the mud flying. Unfortunately, it seemed to have a knack for landing in Jan's mouth.

We needed a taste of civilization before the next leg of the journey. South of Cuba, the Great Divide, according to the map, winds through a maze of terrain with out of this world features like pinon-studded plateaus, deep arroyos, abandoned ranches, and volcanic plugs. The scenery promised to be both spectacular and exceedingly remote. Water was scarce. The route was predominately dirt and did not cross the Continental Divide. This could take three days, maybe two with a push. On the map, it was 116 miles to Grants along Interstate 40.

However, according to the map, should you arrive during a late-summer period of monsoonal rains, which can keep things soaking wet for days at a time, you may be forced to follow an alternative, paved route.

This route, which would cross the Divide several times, was a checkerboard of land, crossing into and out of several Navajo settlements like Torreon, Pueblo Pintado, White Horse, Hospah and Ambrosia Lake (with a name like that there had to be water, right?). That meant there would be stores, running water, and vehicles to flag down if we were wrong. It would take two days to do it. On the map, it was 121 miles to Grants, five miles more than the regular route.

Jan wanted pavement. I wanted dirt.

Yellow-stripers we would become.

We learned that term from Roger and Kathy, the Colorado couple who were also pedaling the Great Divide. It refers to the yellow stripes down the middle of a paved road. The last we had seen of Roger and Kathy was in Summit County, Colorado.

Outside the motel window, Jan saw two familiar bikes without owners.

Those bikes belonged to Roger and Kathy.

So that evening, at a restaurant called El Bruno's, we dined on some of the finest Mexican food we had encountered, drank some of the finest, but expensive margaritas we had come across, and filled each other in on what had transpired since that mountain pass sausage dinner outside of Silverthorne. The pair had taken a detour back to their home and were now continuing their Divide ride.

Conversation drifted to the next leg and it seemed yellow-striping was the route of choice.

It was, as Jan put it, "a compromise over the crap of the past week."

And it didn't require any chocolate at all.

The goal, as the four of us rolled out of an overcast Cuba on the paved mini-rollercoasters of Route 197, was Pueblo Pintado 53 miles away. Between Cuba and that town were at least three markets or gas stations to stop for refreshments. High desert, dry arroyos carved by quick and ferocious rains and flat-topped mesas were all part of the land of the Navajo. The sandy arroyos were no doubt places to avoid during those rains, flash floods to disaster. To ride over a bridge that did not go over water was a strange experience, looking down over something that could have been a raging river was a reminder of how scarce water is in this part of the country.

Other new sites began to appear. Hand-painted signs like the one at the Thriftway Store was a tad odd to these eyes used to those with neon lights or done professionally. Windmills dotted the barren landscape. Not the windmills of Holland, but metal windmills. Their metallic whine when the wind was blowing would become music to my ears as we headed further south. Where there was a windmill, there was water as they were used as pumps to fill stock tanks.

There was another Divide crossing, within sight of a windmill. We did our kiss, head butt, hug thing as Roger and Kathy watched and a couple of cars passed by. Crazy gringos we were. Crossing 18. Yellow-stripers tour.

The pavement was good.

"Mud free," as Roger said.

I had pedaled through Native American land in 1992 and also

during a cross-country bike fiasco in 1979. Just as there were stories of alcoholism, vandalism and drug use, there was also the pageantry of the powwows, the history, culture and people. It was like a country within a country, a neighborhood within a city. It's like turning a corner in Boston and entering Chinatown. You know you're in Massachusetts, but it's another world.

Pueblo Pintado was that way, at least in my mind. Our timing couldn't have been better. Fresh produce was being sold from the back of a pickup truck. Zucchini, Navajo squash, peaches and plums were all purchased and loaded onto the bikes. Bike helmets and lycra met ankle-length dresses and headdresses. At a school, we asked about camping opportunities and were directed to a spot that clearly has to one of the most dazzling places to spend the night along the Great Divide.

A dirt road led to the Chaco Culture National Historic Park and the ruins of massive stone buildings built by the Anasazis maybe in 1000 A.D. Think ancient apartment buildings, two stories high. Layers of flat stone and brick, muted white, red, brown, were there to explore. No water. No facilities. No entrance fee. No tour guide.

For one glorious night, Pueblo Pintado (Spanish for painted village) was ours along with the small lizards that clung to its storied walls.

We camped within sight of the ruins we explored as evening came around. Across the flat desolate land, rain fell in the distance from darkened skies. New Mexico and sunsets are synonymous and it was here the glow touched the land. A rainbow formed and perfection was created if only for an instant. Then another came. The rainbows plus light and shadows created by the setting sun teamed up for a magical show on the face of the ancient rocks.

For me, it was a reminder of a time spent in another pueblo, Taos Pueblo, some six years earlier. I had taken a tour of the pueblo and one of the guides invited me back. For a long weekend, I got an outsiders' inside glimpse of Native American culture at the base of the Sangre de Christo Mountains. Sleeping in the pueblo, going to a powwow and just spending time with a people so different from me, was a wonder and eye-opener.

For now though, my eyes would be shut as the day ended with the sound of galloping horses cutting through the night and under the stars in a land with many tales.

Joggers were not frequent figures along the Great Divide. Beer bottles, yes. Runners no. Come to think of it, Colorado was the state with the most men and women in motion along the roads and trails, running, hiking and biking.

A lone runner was out in the still of the morning and was interrupted with questions about water in the area. Mike was a dorm coordinator at the Navajo Community School in town and that was where he suggested we stock up before yellow-striping up and down Reservation Road 9.

The hot sun was upon the day much too quickly. Tongues were as dry as the sandy washes which cut into the scorched earth. When thirst comes and the water supply is low, the bottom of the throat aches and longs for just a few drops of the life-sustaining fluid. Water was on the brain. Even a stray dog along the road which joined our foursome briefly needed some. Kathy obliged.

Adding up all of our ages, we had a cumulative age index of 189 years. Our ages averaged out to 47. You would think a 47 year-old person would know how much water to take on lonely stretches of a bike trip.

If you thought this, you would be wrong.

Though the terrain in this part of the country was somewhat moderate, we were plagued with strong headwinds. Jan experienced her first flat, the rear tire. Once again, our dead pump was lifeless, even in the hands of Roger. Good thing he and Kathy had one. I couldn't find a bike pump in Cuba and no doubt I would find one in Grants. The fierce winds and heat slowed us down in what we thought would be long, but relatively easy days.

That was wrong.

As the elements played their nasty tricks, the water supply for each of us started to get uncomfortably low. In times like these, you start eyeing the vehicles passing by at 65 miles per hour. If they have an emblem (like a state seal) they are prime targets. State trucks usually carry a huge jug with water in the beds of pickup trucks. So do construction workers.

Unfortunately, this lesson was learned a bit late.

After spotting two construction vehicles with coolers, we figured to hit up the next one. There was a third truck in the entourage. We flagged him down.

He told us the other two trucks had the water. He did give us the water in his 20 ounce bottle though.

Replenished for the moment, we crested a hill and there I saw Kathy and Roger flagging down a police cruiser. The officer and passenger stopped. He was asked if they had any spare drinking water. They also had a couple of 20 ounce water bottles. They offered them to us as they sipped on their quart sized sodas. We took the offering and then the officer asked the question of the day: "Who planned your trip?"

No one spoke up.

Near evening, water was approaching the empty point again. In the distance we saw some buildings in Ambrosia Lake that looked like a factory. When we got closer we saw it was a prison. The lake that was on our map was dried up. Signs warned of no trespassing and possible maladies from sampling any water we might find.

Instead, we found a white SUV parked at a pull-out. We asked the women inside about water. They didn't have any water, but offered us their soda. We passed.

Enchiladas Pintado
(Painted corn vegetable tortilla)
Ingredients:
1 package corn tortillas
1 zucchini
1 Navajo squash (or favorite seasonal squash)
2 tomatoes
1 green chile
1 small onion
2 garlic cloves
1/2 cup olive oil
1/2 pound sharp cheese
Directions:
Dice all vegetables into 1/2 inch cubes. Sauté the squashes, onion and pepper in oil. Add tomatoes and chopped garlic. Add cubes of cheese. Warm tortilla shells. The mixture will be sticky. Place small amount in tortilla. Roll and enjoy.

137

"There is a bar about three miles down the road you know," said one of them.

Like water in the desert, we were rejuvenated. Of course, the three miles was actually car miles which is really more than what any motorist says. But, the bar did materialize at about six miles.

New Mexico's answer to Montana Charlie's near the junction of Routes 509 and 605 was no mirage for us weary riders. Signs advertising retro swill were as glorious as the rainbows from the night before. Inside the maroon bar with the ice machine outside was a dark oasis with dollar bills hanging from the ceiling. Instead of lining up shot glasses, it was water bottles and Mike the bartender served us up water right away.

We were famished and he offered up green chile burritos with corned beef and red chile burritos with meat and potatoes. After we wolfed down the water, we made the switch to other choices of liquid refreshment when it was decided 53 miles was enough for the day and Grants would just have to wait.

Mike let us camp behind the bar by a mesa of striated rock with a multitude of color. Between the day's events and liquid refreshment, a busy bar didn't keep me up that night nor the horses Jan said she heard.

In the morning we topped off our water bottles because there was still about four hundred miles to go and more vehicles to flag down.

Chapter Twenty-two

Grants to Pie Town, New Mexico

Roger Miller may have sung about getting kicks on Route 66, but for me it was a bicycle pump. Route 66 is an American institution and perhaps the most famous stretch of pavement on the Great Divide Route. During it's heyday, it was quite the attraction to travel by car from Chicago to Santa Monica, California, letting motorists get a taste of small town U.S.A. before monolithic highways and corporate chains put convenience ahead of individuality.

Grants looked good from the seat of a bicycle. There was water, water everywhere and plenty of drops to drink. The interstate rolled alongside. Trains came and went. It was virtually all downhill from the Ambrosia Lake bar to Grants and it was time to take a half day rest and trade the tent for a motel within rumbling distance of the trains. Park those bikes in the room and use those legs to walk. Do laundry, catch up on e-mail, stock up with about four days of groceries for the next leg and finally, at the third store I tried, buy a bicycle pump in a hardware store.

On the quiet of a Labor Day weekend Saturday, the four of us hit the road and said good-bye to Grants and Route 66 to head back into the remoteness of New Mexico for a few days.

This wasn't all that easy. Trying to leave Grants, we found

the road ahead was closed. Detours are never fun when you are traveling by bicycle, even early on a weekend when the construction crews aren't out yet. There is no one to ask how far the detour is going to be.

As luck would have it, Jan saw a woman in her yard and went over to ask about the bridge that was out which had caused the road's closure. This was not a bridge over water, Jan learned, but a bridge over railroad tracks. The woman believed the construction wouldn't impede the four of us carrying our bicycles over whatever obstacles may be ahead.

Road closed. Bridge out. Construction area. Hard hats required beyond this point. (We did have helmets.) Despite warning signs, we rolling rebels stuck to the directions on the maps and made our way through the rubble of construction, carrying bikes, trailers, and gear up and over the tracks.

If cycling into Grants was all downhill, then cycling out was all uphill on the pavement which led to the sandstone and lava wonders of El Maplais National Monument. Spanish for "the badlands," the protected area was created by lava that poured out of McCarty's Cone maybe 2,000 or 3,000 years ago. It is home to lava, cliffs, arches, and caves plus Douglas firs which made us feel at home in the hues of red, brown and gray. Cycling along, one was always looking up at the formations.

A short hike to La Ventana Natural Arch, eroded sandstone and the largest readily accessed arch in the state, was in order. Walking into the Cebolla Wilderness, we found shade and sun, stones both cold and warm to the touch.

South on Route 117, which had its share of roadkill in the form of snakes, we cycled along the lava flows. One section, The Narrows, was a 500 foot high sandstone cliff. In and out of the sun and shade we went, leaving the monument for the openness of the grasslands and its hills.

Hills and heat. Heat was king in New Mexico, even a dry heat. Still, it's a hot heat, and heat, dry or not, can pack a punch. The sun beats down hard. But the sun sets and with it come the colors. The full moon rises. There is quiet by the pinion and juniper trees.

There is time to rest until it is time to roll out again and get to Pie Town.

Though we were riding with another couple, it's not always a 24/7 event. Early and late are all relative. The first couple up can pack up and roll out even before eyes are open in the neighboring tent. There is time for togetherness, time for being apart.

Jan and I weren't alone as we rolled out. Three elk, a coyote and lots of dead rabbits were spotted in the still of a Sunday morning. Rollercoaster hills along the dirt were the way to go as we banged out another Divide crossing, complete with kiss, butt and hug, before returning to the hard stuff of Route 603, reconnecting with Roger and Kathy and entering Pie Town.

Pie Town is a community of maybe 63 people. It got that name because an early resident who owned an eatery posted signs along the roadside boasting about his pies. The nickname stuck. That's really not much of a surprise in a state with a community called Truth or Consequences. It does show a funny bone though.

When we were there, the Pie-O-Neer Cafe was open, so we went in, and I said good-bye to the thought of a Bupkis Day even in this sparsely populated stretch of the state. In the 245 miles or so to get from Grants in central New Mexico to Silver City in southern New Mexico, we only saw one grocery store.

Flat Tire Frijoles

Ingredients:
1/2 pound orzo
1 can black beans
2 garlic cloves
1 large tomato
1/4 pound grated cheddar cheese
1 package flour tortillas

Directions:
Mince garlic and dice tomatoes. Cook orzo thoroughly. Drain excess water and add can of black beans, minced garlic and tomato. Reheat mixture and toss in grated cheese. The mixture will be sticky, enabling it to handle well in the tortilla. Fold shell and enjoy.

We dined on the green chile cheeseburgers and BLT'S, and of course, pie for dessert (apple and cherry). Was it the best pie we ever had? Certainly was the best pie we ever had in Pie Town.

But we were less than happy with the limited grocery store selection. Stock was low. There were three jars of jam, ketchup and A1 sauce for sale. Throw in the cartons of eggs and milk and that was mostly everything. So, as we ate the burgers we cut a deal with the cook - we buy the eggs and he hard-boil them.

Inside, we met the former mayor of Pie Town as he munched his breakfast burrito. Luther Jackson once ran the town for 18 years.

"I fired myself," he said about the end of his reign.

Satiated, the moment was brief as Jan returned to a flat rear tire. Across the street was Jackson Park and its padlocked water pump. The tire was patched and water was eventually found.

It was now just over 300 miles to the Mexican border. We got out the last map, number six. Heavy with water and hard-boiled eggs, the next semblance of civilization would be Mimbres, some three days and about 156 miles away through the high and dry land of sun.

Chapter Twenty-three

Pie Town to Silver City, New Mexico

High and dry it was from Pie Town south to Mimbres through the Apache National Forest. The route didn't snarl like a junkyard dog much anymore but the sand made for a fishtail or two.

Even traveling with others, there is a lot of solo time while riding a bicycle for such a long distance. Beautiful scenery yes, but the mind needs to be occupied. Jan started counting the number of cattle guards we crossed. On a Labor Day Monday, a day we crossed the Divide yet again, Jan, to give herself something to do she said, counted over 27 cattle guards.

I talked to cows, telling them to move. Sometimes they did, sometimes they didn't. Tried to ask them about their future as something between a bun, but I never got an answer.

Every song that you ever knew goes through your head too. Not the whole song, just certain parts. Over and over again, they spin in your head over the miles, the same refrain, the same riff, the same internal beat. In the desert, it was America's "A Horse with No Name." I was in the desert sun, my skin was turning red and all I saw were dry river beds.

Water was limited. Stock tanks and fortuitous encounters with humans in pickup trucks were the sources during early September. Think of the name, cattle tanks, stock tanks. They are for cows.

MARTY BASCH

We are not cows. Cows are probably oblivious to what floats on the surface of cattle tanks. They don't see the insects. They don't care about the dead bats. Cows are pretty happy. What me worry?

Not only do we draw water from these tanks, they were also a source of bathing. Please dismiss the thought of naked cyclists jumping off windmills into cattle tanks. This, at least with us, did not happen. We didn't actually bathe in the tanks. Near the tanks is more like it. Camping with Roger and Kathy, we took turns at the tank, each couple doing whatever naked couples on bike trips do when it's their turn to bathe by a tank near the cactus.

Getting naked is one thing to do. Warming up the water with the camp stove is another. Using a soapy washcloth to cleanse oneself from the road dust is a wonderful feeling, getting the grit off the neck, behind the ears and the corner of one's eyes. It was a time to get one's back clean too, with the help of a friend. Though not exactly a rosemary and mint spa body wrap, it's about the best thing you can do with a stock tank when you're cycling a long way to nowhere.

Water was always the topic of conversation. Trucks would stop and motorists inside would ask if we were okay. At the junction with Route 12 - paved roads now became symbols that civilization did exist, that there are such things as grocery stores and showers in southern New Mexico - two families were waiting for some friends. Jan started up a conservation and next thing you know we're topping off the water bottles plus adding a couple of cans of soda and a beer to the load.

South of Route 12 are the Plains of San Augustin. Flat and surrounded by mountains, the area was once site of a vast lake during a time when dinosaurs ruled the roost. The plains are now ruled by creatures of a different sort - the Very Large Array. Forget "Jurassic Park." Think "Star Wars." This army of radio antennas can be moved around since they sit on a y-shaped railroad bed. There are 27 of them, each 82 feet in diameter, and the whole deal cost taxpayers $78,578,000.

What do they do? The party line is this, from the National Radio Astronomy Observatory, "The VLA is an *interferometer*;

this means that it operates by multiplying the data from each pair of telescopes together to form interference patterns. The structure of those interference patterns, and how they change with time as the earth rotates, reflect the structure of radio sources on the sky: we can take these patterns and use a mathematical technique called the Fourier transform to make maps."

Whatever that means. I was hoping we could use them to call for a pizza or something, but they were off in the distance, too far to actually walk over and take a look.

The plains gave way to the butterscotch scent of ponderosa pines of the Gila National Forest along with a rugged range of cactus, grass, spruce and aspen.

Pickup trucks patrolled the forests of the Gila, hunters in search of elk and deer. Up, down and through the twisting hairpin turns they ride scouting for their targets.

More often though, they saw some bikers huffing up the hills. Sometimes they would pass us two or three times in one day.

Sometimes they were curious.

One blue pickup, a huge mother truck which sat four, was a familiar fixture on our route. Finally, it stopped.

The driver rolled down his window and spoke in a thick Arkansas drawl.

"One thing, I gotta know," he said. "Just where the hell are you going?"

"Mexico," he was told.

An arrow of disbelief pierced his being. Recovering, he muttered a few works.

"You got it licked. You got it licked," he said.

It was the first time I got the sense that we were now at the beginning of the end of the trip. Once we made Silver City, calls would have to be made to arrange our pick up. In a week or so, there would be running water, more clothing options, routine again.

But first it was to the Beaverhead Ranger Station with water and a soda machine (bye-bye hope of Triple Bupkis).

During the stretch to Mimbres, we also encountered our mile. It's not really our piece of real estate, but a piece of the trail that

I sponsored and gave to Jan as a Valentine's Day gift in 1998. Basically, it was a way for Adventure Cycling to raise money for the Great Divide Mountain Bike Route.

What you get is a certificate and your name on the map as sponsors of the mile.

Jan's last name was misspelled.

That should have been a clue. I requested a downhill mile.

About half of it was. Mile 2293 to 2294 is just another blip on the Great Divide radar, but it was a big deal for Jan because she was there. She had gotten there on her own steam. She had ridden the miles, grunted up the hills, stared her fear of snakes straight in the face while also seeing the kindness of strangers, the joys of a sunset and feeling the pleasure of seeing an unexpected landscape while rounding the bend.

Soon enough, civilization was reached.

As we entered the funky town of Mimbres we got another surprise. The lodge we had counted on showering in, eating in and getting naked in had closed. We had to press on.

This is small town New Mexico. We met a forest employee at a closed Mimbres ranger station who actually drove ahead to tell the store to stay open for us. At the store, they called the campground to make a reservation for us.

Jan, Roger, Kathy and I never made it to the campground though. Instead, I inhaled some chicken fried steak at the Mimbres Valley Cafe where the waitress called the owner at home to inquire if we could camp in the back of the restaurant.

This was after Jan asked. Talk about a change of attitude since kicking me under the table in Montana after being offered a free place to spend the night.

We could.

This was good.

But in Mimbres, the dogs bark only at night.

And in the morning, the cafe was also the noisy school bus stop.

So we cycled the 20 or so miles into Silver City, knowing the end was near.

Chapter Twenty-four

Silver City to Antelope Wells, New Mexico and the Mexican Border

Silver City was named for an 1870 silver strike. Not only did that put the town on the map, but a notorious outlaw, Billy Kid, grew up there.

The city of nearly 12,000 is on the edge of the Chihuahuan Desert. If Silver City was named today by mountain bikers, a more appropriate name would be Thorn City because it is the gateway to a holster full of flats.

Six days without a shower, we rolled in from Mimbres before noon, passing an old cemetery in Georgetown filled with Spanish and Anglo names and then the deep sculpted Santa Rita mine.

In Silver City, we parted company with Roger and Kathy who were contemplating a rest day. Through Silver City we walked searching for a bike shop to get an idea of what was waiting for us. The shop was no mirage and there we learned that heat and sand waited for us in the final 124 miles to the border. There also was the issue of thorns, or goat heads, that we were warned about from e-mails of riders we had met who were ahead of us. Another patch kit was purchased for thorn insurance.

The Drifter Motel was our base of operations where we washed a rather thick layer of New Mexico earth from our sun-baked flesh. E-mails, phone calls - an all-important one was made to Jan's brother Jim Connell in the suburbs of Phoenix who was going to drive about 350 miles to pick up his sister - and rest consumed much of the afternoon. Jan and I talked about how many days we should take to ride the final leg of the route. She was itching for home - plus we had to take Jim's schedule into consideration - and the decision was made to make it a two-day ride, leaving as early as possible in the morning to ride as much as we could before the sun rose to toast us. On paper, the first day goal was the final outpost in New Mexico's boot heel, Hachita, about 80 miles away. Never mind that Jan had never ridden that far before.

She was now a lean, mean cycling machine and she would take whatever Mother Nature would stick in her path.

The sun was still sleeping when we awoke on Friday, September 11, riding day 67. Showers, a quick live chat on TV back in North Conway, and it was still dark when we left the motel at 6:35 a.m. after a bit of a sleepless night. We were filled with both excitement and pressure at having to be at a certain place at a certain time to meet Jim at the Mexican border on Saturday.

Rolling through a sleepy Silver City, it felt as if the entire first 18 miles were uphill. Pavement made it easier, but that was a fleeting thought as we turned off for the soft, sandy, and sometimes washboarded road through the desert. By late morning we came upon a huge cattle tank, one with a spicket. The desert was like a moonscape, and the water in the tank, reached via a ladder, like a moving sea. There were tall yucca plants, another Divide crossing, cattle guards and plenty of sand for fishtailing. We had to tread carefully on the sand.

Thorn Ranch was a hint. A settlement amidst the isolation, we had come nearly 40 miles at this point and lunched in the fleeting shade of a yucca plant.

We were refueled, but the sand proved problematic for Jan. After the ranch, and in deep, heavy sand, Jan miscalculated a corner and fell on her right side, skinning her right elbow and adding touches of black and blue color to the tan of her legs and thighs. Nonplussed by it all, she dusted herself off and got right back on the metal horse. In a mile or so, she wondered why she was producing all this effort; it was like she was on a stationary bike. The answer was easy. Her front tire was flat.

So, it was repaired.

Then I looked down at my bike before remounting my trustworthy steed.

My rear tire was flat.

We blamed it on Thorn Ranch.

Even with the flats, we were cruising, covering about 50 miles to Separ, an Interstate 10 stop for the motor vehicle set. Buy a souvenir, fill the gas tank, get a cold soda, and move on which is exactly what we did.

Separ's got the sign though. Look up from the wide, sandy path lined with utility poles along the interstate and a green sign is the first solid, manmade indication that the end is near. A green sign has the message that exit 41 is one mile away and with it, Route 146, Hachita and Antelope Wells.

That was the last mile of dirt before returning to black top. Another sign told us it was now 65 miles to Antelope Wells and the port of entry on the Mexican border. Open 8 a.m. to 4 p.m., travel time to get there was an estimated 90 minutes.

That was by car of course.

Yellow-stripers we became. A yellow line ran down the middle of the road between the thin white lines that marked a narrow shoulder.

A crosswind whipped across the desert just in time for the final Divide crossing, the twenty-ninth hill. There was nobody home on this road. No shoulder was needed. The desert was deserted, with dry yellows and greens for miles to see, mountains we would never touch. Crossing twenty-nine was done by a sign saying Continental Divide, an elevation of 4,520 feet. Weeds nodded, maybe even applauded, as for the final time by a Divide crossing, we kissed, helmet-butted and hugged.

This time the hug was a little longer, a lot longer actually as happy tears flowed from Jan.

"It's all downhill from here," I said.

Jan smiled and gave a skeptical, "Right."

We were both tired, the crosswinds, heat and flats taking their collective toll.

Six miles or so later, around 6:30 p.m., Hachita was reached. We found a collection of trailers, a water tower, church (adobe-style of course) and a couple of restaurants.

The Egg Nest was our destination for our final night in the tent. We were quick for ice cream, and about everything else they had including lemonade. We set up the tent outside (they did offer free dry RV parking and we considered our bikes to be recreational vehicles) and headed back inside for dinner. It was Egg City. The couple who owned the place, Marlene and Pat, made decorated eggs.

Ostrich eggs to goose eggs, there were music box eggs, jewelry eggs and wedding ring presentation eggs. Of course, the only eggs I was interested in were bacon and eggs or sausage and eggs or pancakes and eggs.

A guest book of Divide bikers was available for the signing and when the two learned of our names, told us they had something for us.

It was a note on a pink, legal sized piece of paper.

"Hi Marty and Jan!," it read, "Congratulations. Thanks for the encouragement and laughs and quality big kid time. Best of luck to you both. Sincerely, Tiffany."

There were more words.

"Congrats, hope you guys had fun. It was nice meeting you. 45 miles left. Good luck. Christine Winter (the one with ash blonde hair and blue eyes.)"

This was a note from the Massachusetts high school girls!

Other congratulatory words came from Jackie Martin, the rider from New Hampshire. She explained the group would be stopping in St. Louis on the way home to celebrate at Six Flags.

Don't be a stranger, she wrote.

An emotional and exhausted Jan, once again wiped happy tears from her eyes, chowing down on her last Divide dinner which included cornmeal hush puppies which she adored.

By 10 p.m. it was lights out, though there was the parking lot drunk who kept trying to chat up Jan. Eventually he went away mumbling into his vehicle and we went into the tent for slumbering.

A Hollywood script could not have made for a better sunrise. In that story, the two of us would have cycled off, wind at our backs, reminisced through tears of joy about our travels and would have enjoyed a parade complete with balloons and confetti for the final mile.

This was not to be.

We awoke to the attack of the killer goat heads. Think back to jacks of childhood. Now make the ends of the jacks sharp. You've got a goat head. They have an appetite for rubber, and the soles of hiking boots as well, and they were all over our tires. We had parked our bikes smack in their neighborhood and probably had also, unknowingly, accumulated them over the course of the previous day's ride. There were so many, we needed three patches just for one tube. Jan memorialized the day by taking five of the goat heads she pulled from her tires and kept them, eventually placing them in a plastic bag which she has to this day. She suffocated those suckers.

Her rear tire was already flat. Upon inspection, we noted at least a dozen goat heads clinging to the front tire as well. Oh, let's take them out, was the thought.

One by one, the prickly evildoers were plucked away from the rubber. The going was good until we got to one prankster.

That menace got the last word as it was dislocated.

Psssssssssssssssssst!

Now Jan had two flat tires.

My tires were fairing a bit better. The rear one was fine, but the front one was slowly losing air. Pumping it up would suffice for now.

As the day got brighter we spent the morning hovering over the sink in the restaurant dipping the tubes in the water to find the air bubbles indicating a leak. There were many. Our nerves were near the boiling point, spicy like the eggs with green chilies breakfast would be, and weren't helped by the still drunk desert transient who followed us into the rest room to inquire about our predicament. Though he was just trying to help, we weren't in the mood for offering a play-by-play description of our woes.

Jan's tires were repaired, or so we thought. Anxiousness and impatience paid us a visit. Our patch supply was nearing the end.

By 9 a.m., we were on the road, water bottles topped off. Once we rounded the bend past the flying American flag in the cemetery, there was little else to see. A clear blue sky above the horizon, the Big Hachet Mountains were silhouettes as the sun rose to bake us in the desert.

The last 45 miles along New Mexico's State Highway 81 had to be the loneliest stretch of pavement we had pedaled since the Canadian border. Hardly a vehicle passed and when it did, it seemed to be a border patrol car. The cholla cactus ruled the landscape. No shade. Pure heat.

Hordes of large grasshoppers were all over the road in spots. The black and green grasshoppers seemed to be in the midst of a vicious cycle of nature. The insects would be drawn to the pavement where they would be run over. Fellow hoppers would then feed on the flattened shells of their brethren. Then those hoppers would be run over by a car and the process would continue.

Crunchy.

The grasshoppers were also adept hitchhikers, hopping on the trailers for a spell.

They really weren't all that heavy as passengers. But they were very annoying because Jan and I were stopping every few miles to pump up our tires because of the slow leaks we didn't fix well enough before setting out. We were the cycling wounded, deflated but not defeated by those nasty thorns. We pumped and we rode. We passed through Hatchet Gap, slicing between Big and Little Hatchet Mountains. This wasn't a straight shot. The road did some winding through the valley. Had it not been for the stopping and pumping, this road would have put us to sleep right in the middle of the road with the grasshoppers. Border patrol could have just gone around us.

What did produce smiles on a miserably hot day were the mileage markers. The end was near, not a mirage, when the green sign with white letters had a vertical 25 written on it (NM 81 too). With hardly any wind at times, the sound of air being pumped into the tires was the obnoxious song we heard every time we stopped. Every five miles we would pull over and inflate the tires.

The wind did pick up at about the 15 mile mark, a crosswind. It was like Mother Nature was giving us a giant stiff arm, testing us again. Long, lonely utility poles ran along the horizon. The weeds along the road, and only a cyclist could think this, seemed to be encouraging us, nodding up and down as the wind started to howl across the wide open basin.

Five miles became four, four became three, then two and finally one.

The final mile had a twist to it. Next to the sign was a bicycle rim embedded, perhaps with concrete or plaster, in the ground. We took the obligatory photo and then, riding side by side, continued on the last mile. Antelope Wells was the next sign, the road curved to the left. A few buildings were housed in a shade grove. A pair of antennas reached upward.

We did it!

"Stop,

immigration, alto" said the red sign.

So we did.

There was no band, no parade. There were no speeches given or medals awarded.

In the end, there was a Mexican flag flapping in the wind and refreshingly cool water at the plain U.S. border station in the drab desert.

One moment the wheels were in motion, having met dirt and pavement for over 2500 miles from Canada to Mexico. They had crossed the Continental Divide at least 29 times.

The next moment, after the hugs and tears of accomplishment, the bikes, complete with slow-leaking tires, were being hoisted into the rear of Jan's brother Jim's white pickup truck for the beginning of the long trip home. He had, literally, shown up minutes after we had reached that stop sign.

New Mexico, the last leg of the Great Divide Mountain Bike Route, had been mean. Like a pit bull with sharp, menacing teeth, New Mexico took piercing bites at us. For over two weeks, we put up with the bumpy, jostling, rutted and boulder-strewn dirt and gravel roads.

Though the going was rough, it was the people who came along to smooth things out, not just in New Mexico, but in Montana, Idaho, Wyoming and Colorado too.

Of all the people along the route, there is one who unquestionably sticks out. She is love personified, a gentle and giving person who has the wondrous ability to put up with thorns, no matter in what form they appear to her. She completed the adventure of a lifetime.

When she pedaled to the Mexican border and saw that waving flag, her voice quivered with emotion.

"I did it. We did it," she half-whispered, half-cried.

Yes, Jan Duprey did it.

She would do it again.

And she wouldn't mind if I tagged along.

ABOUT THE AUTHOR AND CHEF

Marty Basch is an award-winning writer, lecturer and cyclist who has written widely on outdoor recreation, travel and culinary themes.

A syndicated outdoor columnist, his articles have appeared in *The Boston Globe* and several regional and national magazines. Basch, a Boston University graduate, is also a member of The Explorers Club.

A former restaurant owner, Jan Duprey is a culinary school graduate. She's had articles published in *The Conway Daily Sun*, *Mountain Living* and on the Internet. She has also contributed photos to *The Boston Globe*.

The two live on a dirt road in New Hampshire's White Mountains.